Considering *The Female Man* by Joanna Russ

or, as the bear swore

Farah Mendlesohn

Cover Image © Judith Clute 1985
Cover Design © Francesca T Barbini 2026

Text © Farah Mendlesohn 2026

First published in English by Luna Press Publishing, Edinburgh, 2026

The right of Farah Mendlesohn to be identified as the Author of the Work has been asserted by them in accordance with the Copyright, Designs and Patents Act 1988.

No part of this book may be used or reproduced in any manner for the purpose of training artificial intelligence technologies or systems. No part of this publication may be reproduced, stored in a retrieval system, or transmitted in any form or by any means, electronic, mechanical, photocopy, recording or otherwise, without prior written permission of the copyright owners. Nor can it be circulated in any form of binding or cover other than that in which it is published and without similar condition including this condition being imposed on a subsequent purchaser.

The views and opinions expressed in this book are those of the author and do not necessarily reflect the opinions or beliefs of the publisher and its affiliates. Luna Press Publishing disclaims any responsibility for the materials contained in any third-party website referenced in this work. The author and publisher regret any inconvenience caused if addresses have changed or sites have ceased to exist but can accept no responsibility for any such changes.

A CIP catalogue record is available from the British Library

www.lunapresspublishing.com
ISBN-13: 978-1-915556-64-6

This book should have been completed in 2020, but as we all know, 2020 was a weird year. One of the things that happened to me in 2020 is that my mother died, very unexpectedly, of a rapid onset cancer. We didn't get on terribly well, but despite that we were very close, and closely politically aligned, and it was Carole who taught me that anger was powerful.

To Carole Underwood
1943-2020
Thank you for the gift of the
Women's Press Bookclub

And also...

To all the women to whom I 'loaned' a copy, who told me that they hated it, and then asked if it was ok that they'd lent it to someone else.

'Go little book...'

Contents

Chapter One: Introduction	1
Chapter Two: The Road to The Female Man	29
Chapter Three: Character	56
Chapter Four: The Structure of The Female Man	94
Chapter Five: Argument	127
Chapter Six: Epilogue	160
Acknowledgments	168
Index	170
Russ's Critical Works Cited	174
Works Cited: Secondary Sources	176

The Female Man is….

An angry book;
A laugh out loud humorous book;
An experimental book;
A metafiction;
A bricolage and a palimpsest;
A story told by a ghost;
An exercise in apperception;
An exercise in praxis;
A book with a multiple narrative frames and embeddings;
A story in which everyone is a traveller in time and space and parallel universes;
A story with multiple narrative frames in which *whose frame is dominant?* is in question.
A book written with the assumption that every single sentence mattered, and the way that sentence was written mattered.
A book in which Russ was deliberately responding to critical theory in ways both stated in the text, and responded to by the text.
The Female Man is an exercise in precision and intentionality, and this short book is written with that in mind.

Notes:

Throughout this book, when I am discussing the author, I will refer to Russ. Joanna is a character.

Because *The Female Man* is a very complex text, it may assist to have the book with you when reading this discussion: instead of page references which of course differ by edition, I have chosen to reference to Part and Subsection so that a quote may appear as (5/I), Arabic/Roman as in the Women's Press edition. Other editions use different numerals or text but the numbering itself remains the same throughout.

Chapter One: Introduction

The Female Man has been my favourite novel since my mid-teens. My mother was a member of the Women's Press Book Club, and each month we chose two books each. I was already a science fiction reader, so when they began (in 1985) to publish science fiction, they were obvious choices. In the first package were two Joanna Russ books: *The Female Man* and *Extra (Ordinary) People*. To say I was blown away was an understatement. *The Female Man* was the first book I read that brought together my second-generation, *Spare Rib* style feminism with my genre of choice, science fiction. *Spare Rib* was a feminist magazine in the UK that ran from 1972 to 1993 and is a reminder (if you need one) that not all second-wave feminism was liberal. *Spare Rib* was strident, queer friendly, inter-sectional and internationalist. It started discussions that others continued. We used to joke that what was discussed in *Spare Rib* one year, would turn up in *Cosmopolitan* the next.

In 1986 when I met my undergraduate supervisor at university (Edward James) it was a book that signalled to him that my interest in science fiction was *serious*. When he got the chance to teach it—after I had graduated—he invited me into the class for the day and the session turned into one of those you remember vividly. I have taught it since, in an undergraduate genre class in 2010 and 2011, and the book remains one of those hugely divisive books which is a joy to teach. It is impossible to cover everything that makes *The Female Man* fascinating in one class. It has proved just as impossible in one short book.[1] My book focuses on what has come to interest me most: how *The Female Man* is written.

In case you have come to my book having not read *The Female Man* (unlikely, I know) here is a brief summary. Joanna is an academic, somewhere in New York. She has spent her entire life trying to find a niche. She hated her 1950s girlhood and thought that in academia she would find a home, only to find herself asked to behave like a man in order to compete, and a woman in order to appease. Joanna is watching the TV when Janet is being interviewed. Janet has arrived in New York at a crossing interchange, disappeared and then arrived in the Pentagon. Janet is from a future and a planet in which men have been eradicated/disappeared/died out. Janet sets out to collect her J counterparts. First she collects Jeannine, picking her up from the sidewalk: Jeannine lives in a contemporary New York and America which never saw a Second World War because Hitler never came to power. This America is mired in Depression (as Jeannine is mired in *depression*), and there has not been a Civil Rights movement. The government is still providing entry level work for the unemployed and Jeannine has one of these jobs, as an assistant librarian. She lives in a one room apartment with her cat, dates a man she thinks is ineffectual, has sex she doesn't like, and lives in a dream world of romantic fantasy. Both her mother and brother want her to get married but don't care who to. All three of them are collected by Alice Jael Reasoner. Jael lives in a

---

[1]. I very much wanted to discuss Whileaway as a critique of the Pastoral but there simply was not enough space.

world where men and women are at war, and the gendered stakes for both are high. She takes all three women to her own world to persuade them to act as a bridgehead so that Womanland can attack Manland through other spaces. Jael is an unreliable narrator of her own world. Jael insists they are all the same person and yet not. Jael succeeds only in persuading Jeannine. That's the *story* of the book but there is oh so much more.

There is also the ghost, who may or may not be Joanna Russ the Author, who follows Jeannine, and Janet and Jael and adds in sardonic commentary. Joanna's self-mocking tirades about the world she lives in contain much of the humour. There are the descriptions of pastoral Whileway, and snatches of its anthropology and philosophy. There are the sharply observed scenes of Janet the Traveller, her incomprehension of 1971 American gender performance mutating into the Absurd. Punctuating this is the commentary of the Greek chorus of feminine stereotypes.

The Female Man dances between forms and styles, offering a thought here, a provocation there, bringing it all together at the end in a welter of exhaustion and exhortation. Tom Moylan admired the 'openness of the montage structure and the self-reflexive commentary of the text.' (89). Jean Cortiel suggests that

> 'One level of this complex novel delineates the historical progression from the alienated woman via the feminist revolution to the woman conscious of herself and able to act. However, the novel makes this historical progression ambiguous: each successive stage is in the future, **but not the future of the former stage**' (Cortiel 77). [My bold.]

Time is linear, but 'the novel does not establish *necessary* causalities between events. The worlds are linked by a disrupted and disruptive chronology' (77). You can't get there from here or even, perhaps, here from there.

The Female Man is not a utopian novel, although it has regularly been taught as a utopia and included in books about utopias. Tom Moylan positioned it as a reappropriation of radical utopianism as praxis (89), the first of the Critical Utopias, arguing it 'acts on the need for utopia… It carries itself as a text from utopian assertion to utopian praxis…' (90). Lisa Yaszek, in *On Joanna Russ* notes that Russ addresses the issue of feminist utopias in her 1981 essay 'Recent Feminist Utopias' linking together the work of Wittig, Gearhart, and her own, with that of Mary Lanes' *Mizora* (1887), and Charlotte Perkins Gilman's *Herland* (1915), seeing them as responsive to their contemporaneous women's movements. But *The Female Man*, while it offers the apparent utopia of Whileaway, is too materialist to present it as such; this is not intended as a *perfect* world, and nor is it a world that you cannot get to from 'here': it is a future, although it may not be our future. Russ's four worlds are all to some degree linked to the historical world and to the challenges therein.

The emphasis is less on Jael's plot to embed military stations on each world than it is on exploring the possibilities of personhood open to women in very different situations. The novel relies heavily on parallel world theory and a utilitarian Marxism in which character is malleable to socialisation; Delany has suggested in *Starboard Wine* that it is a critique of or response to, Russ's earlier *And Chaos Died*… (104), which he had criticised for the almost classically homophobic ending of the miserable homosexual,[2] in that it sets out to restructure society for the misfit rather than the misfit for society. It is written, as Delany notes, in 'pyrotechnic prose' (2009) but it is also written, notably, without metaphor.

The Female Man is an act of feminist literary criticism, engaged both with real life and exploring alternative narrative strategies for the fictionalisation of women's lives. Of feminist science fiction, Sarah LeFanu has written, it 'does not follow simply and directly from the literary forms explored by nineteenth-century women writers. It is informed by the feminist, socialist and radical politics that developed during the 1960s and 1970s' (LeFanu 3). This feminist/socialist/radical politics was not only about changing the world, but about changing how the world is narrated, and *The Female Man* was a conscious contributor to this latter argument. In *The Female Man*, Russ sets out to challenge an approach that inserts women into a male world to construct a gynocentric narrative in which the book sets out to answer Joanna Frye's question, 'Can women interpret their own experience or is experience itself always ready to be interpreted?' (Frye 15)—a question which also shapes the later book, *The Two of Them* (1978). The novel also achieves both a collective feminist sensibility and an emphasis on the individual actant: social forces drive character, in a fashion recognisably materialist, but the novel rejects the modernist single 'reality' and 'unidimensional character' or even one 'right plot.' (Frye, 44)

---

2. In *Trouble on Triton* (1976) Delany responds to the same issue by using two characters: one for whom society can make space and who uses that flexibility, and the other who continually blames society for their own discontent and who finds the flexibility uncomfortable.

Subaltern history or literature is history of literature from below. It pays attention to the overlooked, the unchosen. But it goes further than the history from below of social history to consider how historical and narrative models distort and exclude. In the Khatru Symposium Jeffrey Smith asked about women writing 'unrealistic' male characters. Russ wrote, 'Women have a great advantage in inventing male characters... there exists an enormous body of literature written by men, about men... I suspect *in general* women's knowledge of men...is sharper than men's knowledge of women (through necessity)' ('That's a Girl?', 12)

A broadly Marxist and socialist historiography, subalternist critics consider the 'rhetorical and linguistic strategies employed by those in power, in particular colonial administrators' (Gopal 142). The performative elements of *The Female Man*, the construction of the pink and blue books, and the mocking of the cognitive scripts imposed upon all genders, clearly fit into this concept of the subaltern. So too does the effortless use of code switching between the situations and modes employed in the novel (Mandala 39). The subaltern also challenges a fixation on those in power (Gopal 157). This is portrayed in the early interview with Janet, in which it is assumed by the 'authorities' that Janet must be powerful (she is a Whileawayan grunt). But we also see it as we begin to understand the position of Jael, who projects power, but is actually a schemer within her own polity, not a leader. This is the one element of the argument which is constructed between the four characters and is why Jeannine and Jael often appear in much closer relation in the text than any other two characters: while ostensibly from very different worlds, both remain fixated on and responsive to 'the man', locked in internalised misogyny.

Russ is using the masters' tools to dismantle the masters' house (contradicting Audre Lorde, in *Sister Outsider*, 2007) and does so selectively and subversively. Russ's use of the Greek chorus and the playful, ironic language of flirtation, her dismantling of Aristotelian unity and manipulation of time, moving the female characters from the margins of the story to the centre and experimenting with both individual and collective agency, the shifts of focalization from the knowledgeable (Joanna and Jael) to the ignorant (Jeanine and to an extent, Janet), the rendering of all four as both reliable and unreliable narrators of their situation, and of course the use of satire irony and parody to upstage critique and resistance humorously, all demonstrate Russ's virtuosity. The novel's plain prose and often paratactic style, its use of performance rather than metaphor as its principal literary weapon, are intensely *precise* in their effect.

Which brings us to the point that *The Female Man* is a very funny book. Natalie M. Rosinsky in 1982 listed the ways in which it is funny: Russ uses parody to mock the dehumanisation of both genders (see the party scenes); she is part of Adrienne Rich and Helene Cixous's tradition of Medusean humour which attacks the oppression of the ludicrous with laughter. Much of the laughter, as Rosinsky notes, is the laughter of self-recognition, both in the Greek chorus and their litanies, but also when Joanna is trying to dress Janet or coerce her behaviour to a script. However, although Rosinsky is herself from Brooklyn, she does not acknowledge that Russ—a New York Ashkenazi Jew—uses structures of humour that are very Jewish, something I will explore in chapter 5. There is a recognition of the self-oppression of laughter as when Jeannine laughs at her brothers' demeaning jokes. And all of this is contrasted, Rosinsky notes, with the free laughter of Whileaway in which women do not giggle and hide their mouths, but roar with laughter at their own lives, rationalisations and little hypocrisies. *The Female Man* has a Rabelaisian (bawdy) energy, and this is part of its narrative strategy. It simultaneously takes itself very seriously and yet not seriously at all; the book dances the dance that women have to dance to survive, decorating its darts and lances with laughter.

It genuinely surprises me that *The Female Man* has not been more attractive to feminist critics of mimetic non-fantastical literature. Alec Pollak sees *The Female Man* as 'quarantined' (12) in science fiction, and thereby restricted (Marge Piercy in contrast argues that in her feminist sf, 'her imagination is more liberated to follow through on the imaginative premises', x). The quarantining of *The Female Man* is more a comment on the restricted scope of the literary academy—which, until the twenty-first century, did not look to science fiction for examples—than it is the nature or quality of the text.[3] *The Female Man*, for all its power and its responsiveness to theoretical analysis, has not broken out into mainstream literary criticism or mainstream feminist literary criticism. Helen Merrick in the introduction to *The Secret Feminist Cabal* suggests that feminist science fiction has developed parallel to that criticism. *The Female Man* is never referred to by any of the theorists of 'unnatural

---

3. H. Porter Abbot. *The Cambridge Introduction to Narrative* (Cambridge: Cambridge University Press, 2008. Print) is the first general textbook I have encountered that used science-fiction examples as a matter of course.

narratives', those narratives that break either focalization, temporal linearity, or point of view.

Russ consciously identified herself with modernism (see Letter to Susan Koppelman, 173) and was an admirer of Woolf (see the extensive references to Woolf in *How to Suppress Women's Writing*, 1983) and I will be referencing /deploying a number of theorists here who look to the modernist writer Virginia Woolf for models of feminist experimentalist narratologies. Contextualising Woolf in the feminist and pacifist movements of the 1930s, Delorey argues that 'The fictional "I" who narrates Virginia Woolf's novels is thus both the means of inscribing her own specifically female subjectivity and of signalling the end of the imperial subject... an implicitly universal narratology cannot articulate the feminine/feminist specificity of Woolf's narrative structures' (Delorey107). Mezei argues that

'In *Mrs. Dalloway* (1925), by employing a polyphony of voices, Virginia Woolf paradoxically effaces the narrator, who is seemingly diminished by the presence of so many other (internalized) voices, yet she also enormously augments the narrator's structural role as he/she weaves from one voice to the next in a display of virtuosity' (81).

It seems obvious that if there is an heir or successor to Woolf, it is Russ and particularly Russ's *The Female Man*.

The paratactic nature of *The Female Man* may be another reason why critics have not looked to this text as an exemplar. Russ doesn't play word games in this book. There are no figures of speech, no metaphors or similes or neat rhetorical flourishes: although as Peter Stockwell argues, this is a characteristic of pulp science fiction (Stockwell,

86). Russ argued in 1973 ('Speculations: the Subjunctivity of Science Fiction') that 'most science fiction is naturalistic in style; yet there is the oddest kind of play between the sober literalness of tone of such fiction and its implicit ties to actuality' (19).

In a 1969 essay, 'Daydream literature and Science Fiction' collected in *The Country You Have Never Seen*, Russ condemns what she feels is language without real imagery behind it, a form of 'unseeing'; in *How to Suppress Women's Writing*, Russ cites the poet Suzanne Juhasz, who wrote of a rejection slip that suggested her poetry was too straight forward and she should try *denotation*, *synecdoche*, and other figures of speech, 'I and many feminist poets do not want to treat poetry as a metalanguage that needs to be decoded' (*HTSWW*, 117). Her fellow feminist writer, James Tiptree Jr., with whom Russ maintained a correspondence, may have felt the same way: only in a few of their stories, such as 'Painwise' or 'Love is the Plan, the Plan is Death' does Tiptree make the language dance to represent the Other. Elsewhere, Tiptree uses a prosaic approach that allows the writer to lead the reader from wonder to pathos repeatedly, exploiting to the hilt the sentimental and romantic possibilities of science fiction, while retaining the sense of wonder (Mendlesohn, 2023). Russ, as we shall see, uses a very similar narrative strategy. By this, Russ demonstrates a fundamental of writing the fantastic that not all mimetic critics understand: you can write the ordinary in fantastical language, but the fantastical is most estranging when the language used to describe it is ordinary.

Lakoff and Johnson's book *Metaphors We Live By* (1980) offers insight. Lakoff and Johnson argue that metaphor is culture. Your choice of metaphors reveal the bones of your world. A metaphorical *concept* such as 'argument is war', then cascades into the metaphoric language (5), 'Your claims are *indefensible*' 'I demolished his *argument*' (4). Historical fiction writers are very conscious of this: step back even a century and some metaphors don't work; step back a thousand years and some metaphors become impossible. Metaphors and metonymies are therefore, 'not random but instead form coherent systems in terms of which we conceptualise our experience' (41). If Russ wants to deconstruct or interrogate our systems, then metaphor undermines the process. The refusal of metaphor is a challenge to the very cultural coherence, or dovetailing of assumptions and form (Russ *TWLAW*, xi), that Lakof and Johnson argue metaphor creates. Science fiction, Russ argues, analyses reality by changing it (*TWLAW*, xv), or as Stockwell argues, uses the syntax of logical reasoning to challenge the unreasonable, which seems backward until you tie it to this rejection of metaphor. Susan Mandala argues 'Simple definite noun phrases [and the use of 'the']… evoke familiarity for the unknown, ordinary realisations of tense and aspect normalize fantastic events, unremarkable structures instantly establish altered perspectives, and mundane prepositional phrases and adverbials motivate reader involvement' (Mandala 116). Russ leans into this quality of science fiction in *The Female Man*. Yet despite this, the paratactic writing in *The Female Man* still shares a resemblance to that of Virginia Woolf. In her essay 'The Textual Politics of Virginia Woolf's *Mrs. Dalloway*, Patricia Matson writes of Woolf's prose:

> Woolf's textual practice soars and dances like the airplane, shifts and changes like the clouds, and spirals like the dissolving leaden circles of Big Ben's striking. The novel's syntax and sentence structure work against the possibility of a reading aligned with the authoritative dividing and subdividing of the clocks on Harley Street. The narrative is fraught with digressions, delays, forks in the road, and roundabouts; we, as readers, find ourselves continually displaced (Mezei, 1997, 168).

Russ was a huge fan of Virginia Woolf, and *The Female Man* I would argue, deserves to sit alongside *To the Lighthouse* as a masterpiece of modernist writing. But Russ was also a fan of the grotesque, the gothic and the ghost story. In *The Seven Beauties of Science Fiction*, Istvan Csicsery-Ronay Jr. argues for a scientific grotesque which 'comes with the recognition of an embodied, physical anomaly, a being or an event whose existence or behaviour cannot be explained by the currently accepted system of rationalisation. An exception to a fundamental form or evolution cannot be ignored....' (191). As Csicsery-Ronay Jr. also argues that the physicality of the grotesque is fundamentally linked to femaleness, it isn't hard to situate *The Female Man* within the grotesque. Csicsery-Ronay Jr argues that 'The grotesque's metamorphic physicality has always linked it with femaleness' (Csicsery-Ronay 193). 'By far the most frequently developed nodes of the sf grotesque are interstitial beings: creatures in whom two distinct, sometimes even contradictory, conditions of existence overlap' (Csicsery-Ronay 195). *The Female Man* leans into this idea of the simultaneous and contradictory existence of woman: all the Js are the same person (or not).

Yet *The Female Man* also forces the sublime; the 'shock of imaginative expansion, a complex recoil and recuperation of self-consciousness coping with phenomena suddenly perceived to be too great to be comprehended' (Csicsery-Ronay, 146) partaking of its playful nature, while combining the grotesque's sense of taboo.

Who is Joanna Russ?

Joanna Russ is a very slippery character to get hold of. Kate Schaefer's interview (January 8, 2025) noted that she led a very siloed life. Her narrativisation of her childhood and early adulthood is bald in the extreme (we know she was married briefly, but no one seems to know to whom) and the recent biographical summary by Alec Pollak in the new edition of *On Strike Against God* (1985, 2024), which Samuel R. Delany suggests should be read as a non-fantastical and semi-biographical companion volume to *The Female Man*, has added only a little more.

We know Russ was born in the Bronx to lower middle-class Ashkenazi Jewish parents. Both her parents were teachers (which suggests that they might have been second generation or at least arrived in the USA very early), and as far as we can tell secular Jews, although at least parts of her family were religious. We do not know if the family was active in politics, but the Jewish newspaper of the time, the Daily Forward (*Forverts*) was aligned with the Jewish unions, the Bund and to a degree the Jewish branches of the American Communist Party.

Russ's relationship with her parents was poor and by the 1970s, when they were living in Miami Beach, she seems to have had little to do with them. In a letter to James Tiptree Jr (9 November 1973, University of Oregon, Coll 455/Box 73/3) she writes that she spent her childhood, 'pretending to be the good, unreal little girl my parents wanted'; when she broke with them, it precipitated a mental health crisis (letter to Tiptree, 17 May 1974, ibid), but by the mid 1970s a cordial relationship had been established (letter to Tiptree 16 December 1974).

As a child she loved astronomy, natural history and at the age of 12—around 1948—she discovered science fiction, an age typical for many sf fans entering the field (Mendlesohn, 2009), attracted, as she narrates in the Khatru Symposium, to sf because it 'was wondrous, free of the dullness and limitations of what I was taught was Litrachoor at (in high school)' (*Khatru Symposium*, 1974-75).

This was possibly one of the most masculine periods of science fiction, in which the early women writers of the 1930s had mostly ceased writing, and the feminist writers of the early 1960s (see Yaszek) were yet to emerge. Science fiction was dominated by a generation of men who had spent their formative years in a single-sex military.

The science fiction Russ read was the science fiction of the pulp magazines, and Russ never left her thrill of pulp science fiction behind. *The Adventures of Alyx*, which was published in 1976, is a full-on engagement with sword and sorcery, while *The Two of Them* (1978) works with all the tropes of the original *we-aren't-supposed-to intervene-but-what-the hell of Star Trek* (1966-1969). However 'literary' we may consider *The Female Man*, it is absolutely the product of a reader who read Groff Conklin anthologies and 'looked at the stars and thrill[ed] at the idea that there might be life on other planets....' (Davin, 76). Russ was old enough to experience the Second World War but not old enough to participate, something common to her generation and which rendered that war a touchstone of Before and After.

Russ was offered a place at the Bronx High School of Science but was sent instead to the William Howard Taft Public High School. Russ saw this as insanity but Naomi Weisstein, just a few years below, loathed the place and found it intensely hostile to female students, and it is possible that Russ's parents were aware of these issues from conversations in their community. Russ's nascent feminism emerged and was nurtured in high school and then college, first at Cornell, and then at Yale School of Drama (graduating with an MFA in 1960) which clearly fed into the performative sections of *The Female Man*. By the time Russ graduated she had published her first short story. Gwyneth Jones notes that there were a series of unsatisfactory office jobs (5), a marriage of which we know little, and eventually a PhD at Cornell where Russ acquired an instructorship in 1967, and where she attended the influential Cornell Conference on Women in the same year.

By this time Russ was already writing fiction. At the time, the membership of the Science Fiction Writers of America was around 18% female, which as it requires publication for membership is a reasonable reflection of the field. This was lower than the US Census record that suggested around 30% of professional authors in 1970 were female, confirming that science fiction of the period was a 'male' genre. Russ began publishing fiction in 1959, with her first story 'Nor Custom Stale' (*F&SF*), experimented with playwriting.[4] Russ's theatrical experience may have been small but it very clearly influenced *The Female Man* which, at times is actively Brechtian in its breach of the fourth wall, and for all its experimentalism is eminently stageable.

Russ began her reviewing career with *The Magazine of Fantasy and Science Fiction* in 1966 (see James, 2009), and her first novel, *Picnic on Paradise*, came out in 1968. Her first non-fiction, *The Image of Women in Science Fiction*, was published in 1973, although her best known essay collection is the second one, *How to Suppress Women's Writing* (1983). The stories that later were to comprise *The Adventures of Alyx*, came out between 1967 and 1970, and all but three of the twenty-one stories in *The Hidden Side of the Moon* (1987) came out between 1964 and 1975. 'When It Changed' was published in 1972, setting up the first challenge with a highly successful all-female world, and 'The Clichés From Outer Space' was published in 1975 and its mockery of common feminist and anti-feminist tropes was very much part of Russ's argument that, *there were no women in science fiction*, only images of women.

By 1968 Russ was well enough known to be an invited guest at PhilCon (the annual Philadelphia convention). Science fiction writers and fans, although majority male, were generally enthusiastic about women joining their ranks, in a community shaped by Hugo Gernsback's belief that science and science fiction were for all. In January

---

4. Tolkien and Fantasy Blog, 27 May 2013: https://tolkienandfantasy.blogspot.com/2013/05/joanna-russs-version-of-hobbit.html Russ wrote and staged a dramatic adaptation of the Hobbit at Yale in 1957). In *Again, Dangerous Visions*, the introduction to 'When It Changed' states that four one-act plays were staged, as well as a radio play for WBAI Pacifica's New York station in 1967.

1969, Russ spoke at an Eastern Science Fiction Association (ESFA) event. *And Chaos Died* appeared in 1970 and was well received although Delany, by now a close friend of Russ, noted its homophobia. By 1975 Russ was also publishing longer criticism including 'Towards an Aesthetic of Science Fiction' which was published in the journal *Science-Fiction Studies*.

Russ's politics were developing throughout this period. Russ was part of a network of Jewish Marxists and radicals, and her work imbibes of the materialistic critiques of that tradition. We don't know very much about how political Russ's childhood was, although as noted above it was impossible to grow up in Jewish New York without some acquaintance with Jewish Communism and Unionism, but we do have work from other Jewish writers roughly contemporaneous. Pauline Bart, for example, recalled growing up knowing all about Franco and the Jewish Left (Beck, 65-67); Kim Chernin's family were activists who spent time in Russia in the inter-war period and organised rent strikes; and, of course, many of the Futurians—a Marxist fan group—in Science Fiction were Jewish. More specifically, *What Are We Fighting For?* begins with an acknowledgement of Joanna Russ's friend, the Seattle union activist Clara Fraser, co-founder of the intersectional Freedom Socialist Party (1966) and Radical Women (1967), 'whose lifetime socialist radicalism, commitment to bettering the world, political risk-taking, challenging of existing institutions, feminism, and Ashkenazy-American common sense challenged me to write it' (dedication). Russ attended many meetings at the Freedom Socialist Hall with Clara Fraser, giving readings to raise money for union causes (and for Books for Prisoners), but it is unclear whether she was a member of Radical Women herself. When Kate Schaefer (interviewed January 8, 2025) asked her about it, Russ clarified her politics: 'a Trot' (which may or may not be a reference to a party affiliation to one of the US Trotskyite parties) aligned to the trade union movement and the betterment of life for the working class, and convinced that feminism and anti-racism were core elements in any working-class movement. Clara Fraser's critique of Aristotelian logic is worth quoting here.

1. These laws are only true if one assumes the world is something fixed and unchanged. Nothing moves and develops, because motion implies self-contradiction.
2. Formal logic creates impassable barriers between things, but in reality, everything grows out of and into other things: paper into money, and money into paper again; rivers into seas and seas into clouds; bacteria into animals and animals into humans.
3. A can equal not a; formal logic has too rigid a view of identity. The working class for example, is a heterogenous and contradictory mass. In her words, 'a worker is not a boss, but can think and act like one.'
4. These laws present themselves as absolute, final, and eternal. But in reality, everything is relative, interdependent and changing, and as a consequence, so are the laws of governing them.
5. The laws of formal logic cannot explain themselves; they cannot account for their own origin or cause of being.

1, 4 and 5 perhaps resonate most with Joanna Russ's writings and *The Female Man* specifically, as does the style. We see a similar laying down of laws in the performative sections of *The Female Man*.

What Are We Fighting For? also contains a critique of Marxism, and of socialist feminism, in which she challenges the idea that economic inequalities are solely the result of capitalism, pointing to the fight for the family wage which actively sought to displace women from the workforce, and the complacency with which unions accepted the laying off of women and their relegation to the position of a reserve work force ('A Socialist Feminist is a Woman Who goes to Twice as Many Meetings', 210-235).

In the 1970s, writing to James Tiptree Jr., Russ discussed her politics, embracing a Marxist analysis of politics (3 May 1973, Coll 455/B74, F. 3) but noting that 'All my Marxism is 2d-hand' (24 November 1974, Coll 455, B74, F), and of her own attitude to life,

> 'you must steel your heart and become a Marxist, or something like, then you will understand why things are, or at the very least, you will start thinking in terms of power and privilege and money, which are so bloody important' (letter to Tiptree, 16 May, 1975, Coll 455, B74, F6).

'The necessities of business and getting people fed is what's going to change things.' (letter to Tiptree, 12 December 1975, Coll 455, B74, F6), a belief which manifests in the rural-industrialist society of *Whileaway*.

Among Russ's feminist contemporaries, Shulamith Firestone's *The Dialectic of Sex* (1979) is closest in its materialist stance, and its belief in a view of history based on sex itself is the closest match: at times it feels like a map of *The Female Man*. Russ's materialism is perhaps most vivid in *On Strike Against God*, *We Who Are About To…*, and *The Two of Them*, but it shows up in *The Female Man* as well, in its attention to the things that are men's, that they reserve to themselves, as material stakes in the world, and an awareness of class and feeding into feminism. *The Female Man* needs to be read in this materialist context.

In part what the novel is driven by is the idea, posited by Firestone, that "Sex class is so deep as to be invisible… the reaction of the common man, woman and child— '*That?* Why you can't change *that!*'…" (*The Dialectic of Sex*, 11). Firestone argues that while boys in the 1960s split between the conventional and the unconventional, the girls who went with them could never be more than camp followers (35) 'There was no marginal society to which they could escape: the sexual class system existed everywhere' (35) except in Whileaway. It is this challenge that makes Whileaway in 'When it Changed', far and away the best of the female utopias. *The Female Man* is a clarion call to wake up, precisely to demand that women notice the Sex Class dialectic. This is one reason why Russ needs four characters because only in conversation can this understanding develop.

Joanna Russ, like many sf authors, embraced the idea that science fiction is a didactic literature ('Towards an Aesthetic of Science Fiction', 5) and also argued that 'the protagonists of science fiction are always collective never individual persons (although individuals often appear as exemplary or representative figures)' ('Towards' 5).

In Russ's discussion of academic ideology, she writes,

> 'in all these discussions the conversation occurs as if we were in a heaven of abstract discourse in which ideas develop autonomously and influence other ideas without the slightest connection with the real conditions of the lives of the people who are having the ideas, in short without economic class or sex caste or racial caste. It is what I think Marx would call ahistorical talk.' ('Technology as...', 34)

Jeannine, Janet and Jael are very much *situated* in their place and in their time: we learn about their pasts, and how they as representative individuals come to be, rather than their psychology.

We also need to combine this with Russ's Cultural Judaism. Shaviro notes that in the narrative structure around *Extra(Ordinary) People*, the student continually asks *Is that the way the world was saved?* And finally, the tutor responds, '"What makes you think the world's ever been saved?"' I am inclined to see this as a very Jewish attitude. For one thing, Jews are often reputed to answer a question with another question—perhaps because 'questions and inquiry are the mainstay of Jewish scholarship' (Shaviro, 117). But this is also intrinsic to the issue of whether the world has been saved. For something like two thousand years, Jews have resisted and refused the Christian vision of universal salvation (Shaviro). This novel, while about resistance, also resists in the end the notion that salvation exists through alien intervention (G-d). In a letter to Tiptree Jr, 26 February (Coll. 455, B74, F5) Russ writes of her rejection of exceptionalist arguments around Eichmann and other Nazis, 'Maybe being a Jew helps; we have a tradition of being defiantly geocentric rather than heliocentric.' The manifestation of Jewishness in Russ's work will be discussed in Chapter 5: Argument.

Feminism

Russ's feminism has three key strands: anger with men, an anger with liberal feminism, which aspired to men's estate, and which, as this book tackles, set ever more impossible barriers to ever being accepted 'as a man'; and the third is a materialist Marxism which is rooted in her Jewishness (Russ's Jewishness is easily overlooked as we will see later).

Russ's anger with men, is something front and centre of *The Female Man*. It is that anger that led male reviewers to flinch and rail. The book is not written *for* men, something which triggered rage in many male reviewers, who expected to be the audience for science fiction, who assumed they were the centre of the world and the world-future. It is written for women, and it is primarily directed at liberal feminism. The anger in *The Female Man* is not trying to convince male readers. The anger in *The Female Man* is a consciousness-raising exercise directed at the female reader, to bring her into the sisterhood of the furious. The Js are a Greek Chorus and a Consciousness Raising Group made up of the ordinary, the simple, the enquirer, and the sceptic.

Russ's anger with liberal feminism is very clearly expressed in *The Female Man*. First-wave feminism had been very much rooted in an ideology of separate spheres, but it measured its achievements by the degree to which women entered male spheres, and far less in terms of how it either changed the status of 'women's work' or changed women's lives at a day-to-day level. Attempts to tackle issues of maternity leave and maternity health all foundered and advances apparently made during the Second World War were rapidly rolled back. However, it contained within it the sparks of radicalism in the union fights of working-class women for safe working conditions and better wages.

Second-wave feminism was in many ways much more centred around women's day-to-day experiences, but its leadership in the United States was relentlessly middle class and respectable, overwhelmingly white, and again often focused on the aspirations of middle-class women to gain access to the male sphere. Radical ideas about women's experiences were left to the women of the Women's Liberation movement, many of whom came from American-Socialist-Marxist traditions, and Black women from the Civil Rights movement. The key flaw of liberal feminism, as the radicals would come to identify it, is that it believed that improving the access of women to the male estate would fundamentally change the way women were perceived. As Russ and many other women would discover, the male estate was perfectly capable of making room for women, without changing its attitudes one jot. Reading *The Female Man* today, this seems obvious, but in 1971 when the manuscript was complete ('Commentary' 102) and 1975 when it was published, this was a radical challenge to the consensus of the Second Wave and was one of the key insights of the radicals.

The radical wing of the Women's Liberation movement tended to be younger women, with strong familial links to older radical politics (1930s Communism and Anarchism for example), active in other movements, who brought with them skills from other movements, and were often disillusioned by the men in those movements. As Shulamith Firestone noted, 'They found that no one [no man] appreciated their intelligent conversation, their high aspirations, their great sacrifices to avoid developing the personalities of their mothers' (137: see in particular the relationship between Jeannine and her mother); many of their radicalisms, such as the Peace Corps, were considered harmless, and their experiences in the Freedom Rides and the Vietnam Protests radicalised them as much against left-wing men as against their original targets (Firestone 36). The choice to be angry and to make that anger visible is radical in itself. Many 'mainstream' women's movements had striven not to anger men. Lee Horsely noted that Virginia Woolf thought that resistance should go ahead 'quietly and secretly, since it is tactless to criticise your master' (144). One of the skills many brought with them from those movements was an identification with past radical movements that *had* displayed their anger. They weaponised anger to secure air time, and to recognise that angry men responding to the 'wild' statements of radical women's liberation inadvertently 'spoke' to women, (Dow, 61), and in particular spoke to women who were themselves angry and frustrated.[5] L. Timmel Duchamp has pointed out that many younger critics (for example) decontextualise Russ's remarks about housewife sf, ignoring that the stereotype of the housewife was 'a role actively demanded of women and [that] ruined their lives' (Duchamp, 17); 'the

---

5. In 2024, Sarah Gristwood published *Secret Voices: A Year of Women's Diaries*, 'across 400 years of diarists, perhaps the most dominant emotions were frustration and the resolution born of silent fury.' *Smithsonian Magazine*, February 27, 2024.

feminine mystique still had teeth', something the reader sees Joanna rail against in the novel.

Russ is squarely *second wave*, in good ways and bad... her experiences and rage were organised around her own personal experiences—often to a fault. Although *The Female Man* continues to speak to the experience of many women—in a world that continues to demand levels of compromise and duplicity that are both spiritually and physically mutilating from the female presenting—in one respect the book has dated very badly. Joanna Russ in 1971-5 was transphobic. There is a clear statement in the essay, 'For Women Only: or, What is that Man Doing Under My Seat' objecting to the presence of trans women at a women-only event (*What Are We Fighting For?*, 90). *The Female Man* is transphobic: it constructs an argument that 'transness' is forced upon gender-queer men (a modern term) as part of the patriarchal/masculine desire to construct femaleness and femininity in a way that positions femaleness as 'losing' and as 'weak', and sufficiently artificial that a man might be *better* at performing 'femininity' than a cis woman.

This is quite different from the near-contemporaneous *The Wanderground* (1978) by Sally M. Gearhart which positions gender-queer men as a fifth column, encroaching on the new women's utopia and imitating their feminine mind-speech with an aggressively 'masculine' telepathy, but it is aligned with Angela Carter's *The Passion of New Eve* (1977) in which a misogynist is forced to transition, and with Lisa Tuttle's 'The Wound' (1987), which envisages an all-male world in which losing the game of patriarchy sees men mutate physically into women. Russ, Tuttle and Carter (and many other feminists of the period) understood femininity as a patriarchal construct and thus those who appeared to engage with it—femme-cis women, trans women and drag queens (the latter two not to be confused)—as complicit with the patriarchy.

In 8/VII Jael takes our Js into Manland where, we are told, 'Five out of seven Manlanders make it: these are "real men".' Others are the changed, or the half-changed: all real men like the changed, some real men like the half-changed. 'Nobody asks the changed or half-changed what *they* like.' The section goes on to focus on what the half-changed look like, the 'tells' to watch out for, 'the relative size of eyes and bone structure', their calves and knees. The changed are kept segregated, either owned as wives or in brothels; the half changed are secretaries and mistresses. Anna, the half-changed baby haggler, remains punctilious about their gender identity: they are resolutely *Him*.

But it is not clear that these are trans women: they are men brutalised to take the place of the missing women, to be women not in identity but in treatment. In context Anna identifies as a man, preferring the male pronoun (we do not meet the fully changed so we can't comment on that). They are the product of men turning on men, of shrinking the definition of masculinity into a tight space (Anna did not fight back when he was raped, thus he cannot be a man); they are the function of male-on-male anger. They are the ultimate ending of male rage against the female: 'if popular slang is beginning to call them "cunts," what does this leave for us? What can we be called?'/ '*The enemy*,' said Jael (8/VII). But in addition, and reaching forward to chapter 5 and the section on Jewishness, there is still a point of political contact, because in taking on the position of women—willingly or not—Anna is a victim of patriarchy, a sister under the skin, a Ruth to a potential Naomi. If Jael had led him out of there, would he have gone? Modern readers have offered other readings. My own misprision was that on meeting Anna, while Jeannine and Jael are repulsed, Joanna has a mutual recognition of shared oppression, and Janet is as baffled by Anna as she is by Joanna and Jeannine. Amanda Boulter argues. '*The Female Man* suggests that if the "changed" and the "half changed" are impressionists of femininity, then they are no more so than Jeannine and Joanna, who also practise such fakery' (Boulter, 159). They are a function of society not of innate gender identity. For Boulter, the 'eerie sisterliness' between Anna and Joanna and Jeannine can be interpreted as a mutual recognition of shared performance' (160). For David Moles, if we understand this as Jael's perspective and not Russ's, the text 'affords a reading where that character's transphobia is just another dystopian aspect of her timeline' (28 February, Facebook).[6] It is Jael who is the biological essentialist, not Joanna or Joanna Russ. But we can't ignore that there is a serious problem with what Russ constructed in these scenes. In the *Wiscon Chronicles 1*, Russ retracted this 1970s stance, and that means an admission that the *intention* was transphobic.

Joanna Russ's rage and personal experience—that, as Pollak notes, drives the polemic that is the hallmark of second-wave feminism's authoritative and (falsely) universalising

---

6. David Moles, https://facebook.com/mary.a.mohanraj/posts/pfbid02RhiYfmr27Vxq6NJ7b16JRTCb1396Go9b2C7TqH4KCGPrMu35N9k1ihrU5ueZJJ6nl?comment_id=689185776484501&reply_comment_id=1046451616448268&notif_id=1709793086462872&notif_t=commet_mention&ref=notif

'we'—can feel disciplinary of other women (something I experienced myself in the 1980s). I think Mandelo has it right when he argues that it is in the conclusion of *The Female Man* that we can see Russ's motivation, her move from liberal feminism (to which she came in 1968 with her realisation she was a lesbian) to radical:

> 'That sentence [the epigraph] contains a vital motivational truth for the stylistic change from subtle and gentle feminism [although Russ never seems to have been gentle] to aggressive, narrative-shattering dialectics of radical feminist analysis. Speaking like a lady, speaking gently and subtly as society demands, does not work; they do not listen. The only way to make them listen... is to be aggressive, to slam doors on their fingers...' (Mandelo 26).

Yet, as Shaviro argues, there is evidence in much of her work and particularly in the 1984 short story, 'Everyday Depressions' (in *Extra(Ordinary) People*), that Russ framed herself as what we would now call an intersectional feminist but which for Russ was rooted in and encompassed by her materialist feminism. Discussing a proposed (non-existent) novel, the character/Russ writes to her 'reader' that the book should be full of politics, and then one by one dismisses the different theoretical positions each as inadequate, concluding that she desires a: 'Marxist-Leninist academic lesbian feminist socially culturally anarchistic separatist anti-racist revolutionaries? Too few?'

Chapter Two: The Road to *The Female Man*

The Female Man did not come out of nowhere: there had always been, as we are wont to say, a women's movement, and first-wave feminism had been important to early magazine science fiction (see work by Justine Larbalestier and Lisa Yaszek who have led the rediscovery and re-evaluation of many female sf writers). But as Sam J. Lundwall had noted, science fiction had been remarkably poor at social extrapolation (Yaszek, 33).

The magazine editors of the 1950s seem to have been less welcoming to female writers than their 1930s predecessors, as the 1950s generally were less welcoming to ambitious women (see Eric Davin, 2006, for relative figures). 1967 saw the formation of Women's Liberation movement groups in major northern USA cities, and in Toronto (Mexico in 1970), but even Judith Merril, who might be expected to be sympathetic, was hostile to the new women's liberationists (Newell and Tallentire explore this more closely, 2009) and did not herself embrace the term feminism, which explains the antagonism that Russ sometimes expressed towards her. In contrast we know that Russ attended women's liberation groups and consciousness-raising sessions. Researcher Nichole Rudick notes that there are complaints in her papers about these events which she found facile (personal correspondence, 27/Feb/2022).

Many of the male fans of the 1960s and 1970s, however liberal they saw themselves, were quick to accuse the feminist writers of man hating (then, as now, the practice of sending fanzines to anyone mentioned in them ensured they could be used as a means of harassment). Russ had an unpleasant interaction with Richard E. Geis when he sent her a review by Michael G. Coney of 'When it Changed' (Merrick, 49). A discussion of the book in the magazine *Vertex* overflowed into the fanzines. Many of the letters in Richard Geis's *Psychotic/ The Alien Critic/Science Fiction Review* (same fanzine with different names) were intensely personal.

Although we can identify women's issues authors in the early to late 1960s—what Lisa Yaszek called, without disparagement (unlike Russ herself), the writers of *housewife heroines* (of which the most radical may be Pamela Zoline's 'The Heat Death of the Universe', 1967), assertively feminist work appears only at the very end of the decade with Le Guin's *The Left Hand of Darkness* (1969)[1], and Monique Wittig's *Les Guérrillères* first published in French in 1969, and translated (badly) in 1971 when Russ was completing the manuscript of *The Female Man* (Commentary, 102). We know Russ disliked *The Left Hand of Darkness*, expressing an acute gendered critique of it which others shared (Newell & Tallentire, 74), and we also know that Russ wrote *The Female Man* before she had read *Les Guérrillères* (1969). On the other hand, when she did read it, she thought that *Les Guérrillères* was wonderful. Angelika Bammer described

---

1. In Russ's review of *The Dispossessed* (*The Country...*, 110-113), Russ expresses her frustration with how very skin-thin Le Guin's feminism is: 'we are told that Anarresti children copulate with each other bisexually...[yet only see heterosexuality].We are *told* near the *end* of the book that it is common for the father to be the child's nuturing parent; yet Shevek, the hero, suffers from his mother's absence...' while he walks away from his child, Russ continues. Fifteen-year-old me would have loved to have read this review.

Les Guérrillères as less a utopia than a 'constant process of reworking the very cultural scripts into which we are not only written ourselves but which we participate in writing' (7) and a text of rage (124) which seems also to describe *The Female Man*, whose performative sections are direct challenges to the cultural scripts. Russ did see it as a utopia, both 'raw' and 'brilliant' (*How to Suppress*, 130).

Joanna Russ's radical feminism emerged along with that of others in the women's liberation movement. By radical feminism in this case, I mean one which is both materialist and convinced that 'Maleness or femaleness is among the most important concrete, specific data of a human being's situation and to write authentically one must write from a concrete, absolutely specific history' ('Gimmicks are Not enough', 60). Russ qualified this in the same piece, pointing out that everyone carries qualifiers of race, age, and experience. But it is in this context that we should understand that the regular accusation against *The Female Man*, which we will examine (and not exonerate) in chapter 5, is that it is transphobic. I don't know if Russ was at the West Coast Lesbian Feminist Conference in 1973, but it was there that Robin Morgan asserted her lesbian identity, its importance to feminism, and challenged the split between lesbian and straight women. One of the major events of the conference was Morgan's hostile challenge to Beth Elliott, a folk singer and a transsexual woman who had served as the vice-president of the San Francisco chapter of the groundbreaking lesbian group The Daughters of Bilitis, from 1971 to 1972, and editor of the magazine *Sisters*, and one of the organisers of the conference, so in effect, one of Morgan's hosts. Morgan refused to recognise Elliott as a woman. The

Gutter Dykes, a Lesbian separatist group, heckled Elliott at the conference: when allies (Jeanne Cordova, Robin Tyler and Patty Harrison) forced a vote it resulted in something like two-thirds of the conference supporting Elliott. Despite this, Morgan made binary essentialism a cornerstone of her speech the next day. Morgan referred to Elliot as a 'gatecrashing... male transvestite', repeatedly used 'he' and accused her of being 'an opportunist, an infiltrator, and a destroyer—with the mentality of a rapist' (https://en.wikipedia.org/wiki/Beth_Elliott).[2] In 2006 Joanna Russ repudiated such views (which strongly suggested she had held them) in an interview with Samuel R. Delany Jr., conducted on the telephone at Wiscon: 'it's almost as if my life has arranged itself to disabuse me of one prejudice after another. And all of these have gone because none of them were real, really.' In the analysis that follows however, I will offer critics' interpretations, while accepting that Russ (and myself) swam in a transphobic bio-essentialist feminist environment in the 1970s and 1980s.

The next few years saw feminist science fiction from some of the now biggest names in the field (often their first novel). Suzette Haden Elgin published *The Communipaths* (1970), starring a James Bondish adventurer through cultures which challenged the heteropatriarchal norm. Octavia Butler published her first short story ('Crossover'); Marion Zimmer Bradley[3] published *Darkover Landfall*

---

[2]. Robin Morgan, 'Keynote Address' *Lesbian Tide*. May/Jun73, Vol. 2 Issue 10/11, pp. 30-34 (quote p. 32); additional coverage in Pichulina Hampi, Advocate, May 9, 1973, issue 11, p. 4].

[3]. The revelations that Bradley was a child abuser and a facilitator of child abuse has been traumatic for fans, but here I am focused entirely on contemporary responses.

(1972) which feminists *hated* for its re-enslavement of women—Russ engaged in a conversation with Bradley over its sociobiological premise in *The Witch and the Chameleon* (1974-1976) (Merrick 59)—, and which Russ may well have been responding to in her 1976 *We Who are About To...* (Bradley waited until 1976 to challenge patriarchy with *The Shattered Chain*). Pamela Sargent edited *Women of Wonder* in 1974, retrieving many earlier voices, and in 1976, Vonda N. McIntyre and Susan Janice Anderson published the consciously feminist, *Aurora: Beyond Equality* (which was meant to contain four stories by men and four by women, but two of the stories were by Alice Sheldon under the Tiptree and Sheldon pseudonyms). A history of women's publishing in the 1970s and 1980s, can be found in Sarah LeFanu's *In the Chinks of the World Machine* (1988).

Many of the famous feminist utopias are also relatively liberal pieces.[4] Among the radicals Suzy McKee Charnas's *Walk to the End of the World* (1974), James Tiptree Jr's 'The Women Men Don't See'[5] and Russ's *The Female Man* (1975) along with Marge Piercy's 1976 novel, *Woman On the Edge of Time*, and Wilhelm's *Abyss: Two Novellas* (of which Russ noted, it lacked 'the feminine mystique', James, 25), all stand out for their utter lack of compromise with the patriarchy. Although Hicks argues that you can understand the monologues in *The Female Man* as a response to *The*

---

4. Jones: 'Even in nineteenth-century America, female utopians found the conviction that a woman's story ends with a wedding hard to shake' (55), and argues that the sf utopians such as Lilith Lorraine (no other examples are given) put their trust in political and social advancements 'without challenging male dominance directly' (55).

5. James Tiptree Jr. was still thought to be a man but the radicalism of this story brought it marked attention.

Feminine Mystique's assumption that the right to high status work is 'a virtual panacea for their discontents' (1999), each of these four titles is clearly linked less to the Women's Movement as a whole than to radical Women's Liberation, with its roots in socialism and anti-racism.[6] For the utopian scholar Tom Moylan, *The Female Man* was the first of the 'critical utopias', responding to capitalism's apparent post-war victory (41) counterposed in Jeannine sections, and constructing 'utopia as struggle... a walled effort to transform the social system'. Angelika Bammer, who divides the feminist utopias into a number of groups, classifies *The Female Man* as one of those that 'situate utopia not in a separate or separable sphere outside of existing reality, but on the boundaries where the real and the possible meet, where resistance creates room for alternatives (Bammer, 7): it is a fluid text which is less a utopia than it is a demand for utopia. And it's not clear that Russ would have been comfortable with the idea of *The Female Man* as a utopia. Of academic conversations on the topic of technology, she wrote in the 1980s,

> 'in all these discussions the conversation occurs as if we were in a heaven of abstract discourse in which ideas develop autonomously and influence other ideas without the slightest connection with the real conditions of the lives of the people who are having the ideas, in short without economic class or sex caste or racial caste. It is what I think Marx would call ahistorical talk' ('Technology as...', 34).

---

6. Tiptree is the oddity in that Tiptree's work is littered with racism that cannot be assumed to be the character's voice.

In this Russ is clearly post-modern: Pamela notes that 'If we attend to the stories postmodern writers tell us, we realize that there is no end goal toward which we are progressing, no common ground on which we can rest' (xiii). Distinguishing post-modernism from feminism, Hutcheon writes: 'feminisms are not content with exposition: art forms cannot change unless social practices do. Exposition may be the first step, but it cannot be the last' (Hutcheon, 1988, 263). What feminism brings to the table is that it theorizes agency (Hutcheon, 1988, 266).

Alongside these developments was the emergence of sf criticism by feminists. Joanna Russ's own essays, the collection we have already mentioned, and Amelia Banker's *The Witch and the Chameleon* (1974-1976), which Russ contributed to (Merrick 2009, 59), are all likely to have been on Russ's reading list and collectively contributed to a sense that there might now be space (and readers) for a novel as radical as *The Female Man*, which did not just critique the patriarchy, but which stepped outside the private sphere which Yaszek identifies as the setting not only for the 'housewife' authors, but also for Russ's early stories (2009, 47). *The Female Man*, although it is often listed among feminist utopias, is, in ways that are explored in chapter 3, better understood as a critique of feminist utopia.

As feminist science fiction flowered in the 1970s, so too did feminist science fiction criticism. Yaszek asserts that Joanna Russ more or less singlehandedly created feminist sf scholarship (Yaszek 35). This I feel is to repeat the very mistake (for which Yaszek accuses Russ) of dismissing earlier feminist sf scholarships, but it does draw attention to the issue that *The Female Man*, while fiction, is clearly also feminist sf critique (as Wolfe also argues are the Alyx books). One of Russ's contentions was that feminists had to develop feminist critical tools. In the introduction to a letter to Susan Koppelman, reprinted in *To Write Like a Woman*, Russ argues that 'Anyone who seriously tries to make received ideas [Lacan in this case] do feminist work will find that the received ideas end up making her feminism to *their* work…' (171).

As a reviewer, Joanna Russ was acerbic and witty. Gwyneth Jones argued that whereas Judith Merril in her reviews would link her chosen texts thematically, Russ 'took the riskier approach of *criticizing* science fiction: applying the analytical skill, the patience (and the cutting wit) of a demanding teacher' (25). But reading the collection in *The Country You Have Never Seen* (2007) the reviews stand out more for their entertainment value than for their insight; they are simply too harsh and hard-hitting to be useful as criticism. However, in the same collection are Russ's reviews of new feminist critical works and one or two fictions (by Piercy and Le Guin) and here it's worth considering Russ's comments as evidence of what she herself wanted to achieve and wanted to see achieved. The collection includes reviews of Shulamith Firestone's 1971 *The Dialectic of Sex* (62-67), Jessie Bernard's 1973 *The Future of Marriage* (186), and Mary Daly's 1979 *Gyn/Ecology: the Metaethics of Radical Feminism* (155). In these book reviews, some written before, some after *The Female Man*, we can I think see Russ recognising herself (in contrast to the outrage she expresses when she says 'there are no women in science fiction, only images of women' in which she does not recognise herself).

For Russ, perhaps unsurprisingly, Firestone's *The Dialectic of Sex* (1971) was 'the most exciting social extrapolation around', an answer to the poor record of science fiction. She picks a number of highlights, several of which focus around dissolving the distinction between the personal and the political; several more around the deconstruction of the family, and the dissolution of distinction between child society and adult society (63). Russ dislikes Jessie Bernard's *The Future of Marriage* (1973) because it is obsessed with functionality and with dualistic model of marriage that presumes that gender is the core identity, and presumes that the number of people in a marriage makes no difference. Dr Bernard, like many of the male sf writers Russ demolishes, is guilty of monolithism, a 'comfy timelessness', a very poor anthropology that Russ seeks to demolish/challenge.

Daly's *Gyn/Ecology* attracts Russ I think for the same reason Firestone does, because her work is angry and takes no quarter, 'a while, whirling, terrifying, ecstatic, haggard book (155) engaged in a 'mythic reclaiming of the cosmos for women' (156). '*Is Daly trying to start a war?*' Russ asks, and responds to herself, 'But the war is already going on...' (157). And lists the ways in which horrors are rendered lesser through naming. Oddly, Russ claims she does not understand why Daly argues that 'femininity' is a product of patriarchy, '*a male projection of a solution to problems in the male situation which is then imposed on women*' (158), because this *is* the argument of *The Female Man*.

Prior to the publication of *The Female Man* Joanna Russ had produced a number of short stories, several of which were later included in *The Adventures of Alyx* (1976) and just two novels, *Picnic on Paradise* (1968) in which Alyx is hired from Earth's past by the Trans Temporal Authority to rescue stranded travellers, and *And Chaos Died* (1970) in which an Earth man lands on a planet of telekinetic people, acquires that telepathy and returns to Earth, trying to cope with it. The book is not of much interest for its plot (and its sexual politics, which link homosexuality with misogyny, are dated), but it is of interest for the experimental nature of the relating of telepathy. Russ's depiction of telepathy is very different from that of most of her contemporaries (and telepathy was one of the science fictional fads of the 1970s), it depicts not easy communication, but an attempt to imagine what telepathy might really be like given the random nature of many people's thought processes. Thus where Alyx may be a prototype Jael, Jai's thoughts in *And Chaos Died* may be a prototype of Joanna's meta narratives and the novel's structure.

Gwyneth Jones points to a number of extracts from *The Female Man* which saw print before the novel (53-54). Collected in *The Zanzibar Cat* there is 'Gleepsite' (1971, Orbit 9), in which after the war between Manland and Womanland is concluded, Jael and Joanna visit empty offices and give the watch ladies they find a way out; 'Nobody's Home' is about a world in which super-fast travel (teleportation) and communication has reduced the world to a shallow party but which contains the computer-helmet automation, and 'An Old Fashioned Girl' in *Final State* (ed. Edward L. Ferman and Barry Malzberg, 1974), an extract from part 8 of *The Female Man* (but of which Jones says nothing). We can see snippets of some 'Joanna's' memoirs in the essays in *Magic Mommas, Trembling Sisters, Puritans & Perverts* (1981).

Of course, the piece of work that *The Female Man* is most attached to, is the short story 'When it Changed', published in *Again, Dangerous Visions* (1972). One of forty-two stories in Again, Dangerous Visions—a collection that included such then luminaries as Kurt Vonnegut, Ursula Le Guin, Gene Wolfe and Thomas M. Disch, and now luminaries as M. John Harrison, James Tiptree Jr., and Ben Bova—the story is probably now the only short story in the collection (Le Guin's *The Word for World is Forest* is not a short story) to invite instant recognition. It won the Nebula for best short story in 1972 and was a finalist for the Hugo Award in 1973. The joint winners of that Hugo have long since been forgotten.[7]

LeFanu describes 'When it Changed' as

'all of a piece with the early days of sixties and seventies feminist consciousness: the bold simplicity of the parameters; what seemed like the sudden glaring obviousness of male op-pression; the ease with which men can be mocked and the danger of doing so' (185).

It is a completely linear, first-person story of existence in a frontier society. Although Joanna Frye argues that the use of first person can be seen as a radical act: 'Once the female "I" has been spoken, the subversion is begun—

---

7. 'Eurema's Dam' by R. A. Lafferty [*New Dimensions* #2, 1972] (winner)

'The Meeting' by Frederik Pohl and C. M. Kornbluth [F&SF Nov 1972] (winner)

'When We Went to See the End of the World' by Robert Silverberg [*Universe* 2, 1972]

'And I Awoke and Found Me Here on the Cold Hill's Side' by James Tiptree, Jr. [*F&SF* Mar 1972].

'When It Changed' by Joanna Russ [*Again, Dangerous Visions*, 1972; Sci Fiction, scifi.com 2000-11-15] even in novels embedded in the patriarchal context, even in novels by men'(50). The story as a whole has nothing of the dizzying experimentalism of *The Female Man*. For all the surface links of planetary name and of the main character, it is a literary world away from its successor. The Janet in 'When it Changed' is a much nicer character than the Janet of *The Female Man* even while she is engaged in the transgressive role of police officer.[8]

There is no need to dissect the plot or themes of the story because it is well known and easily available, and Sarah LeFanu does it very well in *In the Chinks of the World Machine* (1988), but in the context of this book in which narratology trumps plot, I want to think about how Russ has chosen to structure the story. It is in first person, at a time when that was less common, and Russ makes use of the full hermetic seal of the first-person narrative; the narrative is intensely visceral with Russ emphasising the narrator's feelings and responses and situational experience. The narrator is also fully fleshed: we can construct her in our heads as the more restrained, and more wary member of her marriage. She may have fought three duels but 'I am afraid of far, far too much.' It is Katy who brings exuberance to their marriage, but this is no monolithic culture, even then, the protagonist is too flamboyant, too *southern* for Lydia, the district biologist.

The first-person visceral narrative also shapes how we learn to see the earth people as alien, as *wrong*. For Janet

---

[8]. Even today, the USA has a far lower ratio of women to men in the police force than most western countries, at 13% compared to the UK's 35% and Australia's 50%—in part, one must presume, because of the violent framing of the role, given that 70% of civilian police roles are filled by women.

the visitors are *off*: 'apes with human faces'. For Yuki, her daughter, the visitors are exciting interventions in the world. Towards both Katy and Janet the visitors are dismissive, reducing their roles, 'some **sort** of chief of police' (my bold); they make assumptions (that the marriage is merely a contract not a loving sexually active engagement, that Katy is the femme, that she would 'benefit most' from the arrival of male humans). The story closes where it began with a story of fear, but moves from fear of one's own context to fear of and Out of Context Problem,[9] from containable fear to that fear that all women share, the fear men will laugh at them *and* kill them. But Janet, who is not the Janet of *The Female Man* also notes, 'Katy was right, of course; we should have burned them down where they stood.'

The reaction to 'When it Changed' was mixed, as might be expected. LeFanu argues that, the

> 'Russ short story, "When it Changed"... seemed to have a special resonance for women readers, and is regularly favoured over what Russ herself calls her "feminist novel" *The Female Man*, where Whileaway reappears, but in a quite different context from the unproblematic "When it Changed"...' (LeFanu 175).

By the time it reappears in *The Female Man*, it is not actually a utopia as such, even if it appears utopian to us. 'When it Changed' can be seen as essentialist story (LeFanu 185) in which women are good and men are bad; although I am not myself convinced of this: I think Russ argues in

---

9. Iain M. Banks, *Excession*, 1996.

'When it Changed' that women on their own are *whole* in a way familiar to those of us who read English girls' school stories from the early twentieth century, or Nancy Drew, and that men are damaged by the assumptions of unequal societies. Russ wrote,

'I believe the separatism [of the feminist utopias] is primary, and that the authors are not subtle in their reasons for creating separatist utopias: if men are kept out of these societies, it is because men are dangerous. They also hog the good things of this world' ('Recent Feminist Utopias', 140)

This is also the argument made in *You're a Brick, Angela!; The Girl's Story 1839-1985* (1986) by Mary Cadogan and Patricia Craig.

The virulence with which some male readers reacted to it at the time was intense. Helen Merrick's article, 'The Female 'Atlas' of Science Fiction?" (2009) goes into this in some detail. The chief prosecutor was sf author Michael G. Coney with a letter in the pages of *Alien Critic* (2, no, 3, 52-53) in which he argued that women's liberation was just a topical bandwagon and that the story was merely one more experiment in 'the-majority-is-a-bastard' stories. Like representatives of man-movements today, he felt attacked 'by every crank under the sun' for the crime of being a white, non-religious heterosexual male. For Coney, this rather mild-mannered story reeked of 'hatred' and 'destructiveness'. Merrick argues that Russ's socio-political arguments are refigured by Coney as biologically determined (50). But I am not quite so convinced that Coney is wrong; as I will discuss later, in *The Female Man* there is a bio-essentialism that trumps her Marxism, but it is a subtle form in which bio-essentialism is pluralistic, not monolithic.

The Publishing History of *The Female Man*

Russ began working on *The Female Man* in 1969 and finished it in 1971. It took four years to place but was read by several of her peers in manuscript (Moylan 57) including Marilyn Hacker, Samuel Delany and Ursula Le Guin. In a letter to Cortiel, Russ reported that this was due in part to her agent's attempt to sell it as a hard cover (Cortiel 57): it was finally published in hard cover in 1977 by Gregg Press. The first printing was thus by Bantam in a cheap paperback edition of the kind that one found in drugstores. Bantam reprinted it in 1978 with an abstract cover associated with more intellectual science fiction, and in the 1980s it was picked up by the Women's Press in the UK, then Easton Press, Beacon Press and Goldstone. By this time it was appearing as a trade paperback. The general impression has been that this book was relatively hard to secure—and it did go out of print periodically—but there is a US edition in every decade, and from 1985 the same in the UK. Most recently it has been taken up into the Gollancz Masterwork collection, thus ensuring it won't go out of print easily. The novel was also translated into French, Dutch, Italian, German, and Spanish, *The Female Man* has attracted consistent interest, even while it has never been a best seller.

The Female Man was first drafted in 1971 (Russ, 1975, 79; Jones, 41) and was written as Russ wrestled with ideas of *what a heroine can do*, also the title of an essay she published in 1972 and wrote after attending a symposium on women, hosted by the School of Home Economics in Cornell,[10] at which Betty Friedan and other prominent feminist thinkers were attendees, and which shook her world (1975, 79). At the start of the essay Russ lists eight plots of which, for brevity's sake, I will list only the shortest.

> 1. Two strong young women battle for supremacy in the early West.
> 2. A young girl in Minnesota finds her womanhood by killing a bear.
> 7. A young man who unwisely puts success in business before his personal fulfilment loses his masculinity and ends up as a neurotic, lonely eunuch.

All of these, as she notes, were common plots of the time, only—excepting the final example—with male, not female, protagonists. The ludicrousness of the role reversals in 1975 (today I might be able to find titles that matched these outlines) for Russ drew attention to the problem that 'Culture is male' (80). And that what this means is that almost all imaginative culture is from the male point of view. 'There is a female culture, but it is an underground, unofficial, minor culture…' ('What Can a Heroine Do?…' 81), so minor that even women are slow to use it. It was hard to find: in 1971 Russ could not find an in-print edition of Charlotte Bronte's *Villette*; when she said she was teaching

---

10. The history of Home Economics Departments in the USA is fascinating. They were used to sideline women—chemistry for food processing—but like other conservative women's space, sheltered a nascent radicalism. See https://olinuris.library.cornell.edu/past-exhibitions/parallax/russ/the-female-man for a reference to the conference.

Jane Eyre, she was dismissed as being interested in 'the minor Victorians' (*How to Suppress*, 63, 46).

In 1971, *Literature* was not about men and women, it was about men. So when we wonder why it took four years for *The Female Man* to be both written and then published (in 1975) it may be that Russ first had to work out what women's stories could be told that were more than just subversions of men's stories (as are the adventures of Alyx in the book of the same name), and also for the culture to begin to shift, or at least, for woman culture to get not bigger perhaps, but louder and more demanding, and for there to appear not just story-tellers but myth-makers from the feminist community. As Russ noted, 'one of the great pleasures of the 1970s was finding so many other women doing so much fine work on so many things' ('My husband's trying to kill me…' in *To Write Like a Woman*, 94).

The Khatru Symposium took place in the same year (September 1974-1975) as the publication of *The Female Man*. It is famous for having included James Tiptree Jr. prior to their 'unmasking', but it is also notable for being a space in which the radical feminists took the lead, and Russ expressed her anger with the day-to-day experiences of existing as a woman in a male space (academia). LeFanu points out that Russ's novel *We Who Are About To…* was written in the same year as *The Female Man* and published in *Galaxy* in the same year that *The Female Man* was published (177): yet despite being, in some ways a more *punitive* book, and a profoundly nihilistic one, which argues that individual human lives are worth very little, it has never attracted the outrage that has *The Female Man* (this may change soon as the hostility to the choice to keep a disabled child alive, at great expense, runs counter to current sensibilities).

Reactions to the Novel

When *The Female Man* was released, sf criticism and the sf fanzines were still predominantly a man's world so that we cannot think in terms of majority and minority responses. Marilyn Hacker had advised Russ that the flaw in the original ending of *On Strike Against God* was that it was addressed to men, not to women (Pollak, 33): *The Female Man* never makes this mistake. Many male critics either missed the point that they were not the intended audience, or understood it and resented it.

Richard Harter, in his fanzine *Harter's World* (1976), wrote that Russ was a crank and a bad writer. Michael Goodwin in *Mother Jones*, a radical magazine, said that *The Female Man* was 'a scream of anger' and 'a bitter fantasy of reversed sexual oppression' (qtd in Russ, 'Recent' 144). Lester Del Rey wrote in *Analog* (June 1975) that it was 'an angry book that turns first to rage and winds up in fits of jealousy and hate. It's a wish dream of vengeance, a vendetta against all the male half of mankind' (168), and that only those who already disliked men would like it. Cory and Alexie Panshin also disliked it (*The Magazine of Fantasy & Science Fiction*, August 1975). Edward James, a fan of *The Female Man*, remembers being angry that Rog Peyton, owner of the Birmingham UK science fiction bookshop Andromeda, refused to stock it because he detested it so much.[11]

---

11. Edward James, personal conversation, 5 May 2025.

Janis Kelly, in the radical magazine *Off Our Backs*, clearly liked the book, describing it as ahead of its time (1975). So did Susan Wood, science fiction fan and convenor of the first Women in SF panel at the 1974 Worldcon (Merrick, 55), but she did not like the polysemic nature of the novel seeing the lack of Aristotelian unity as a flaw, and regarded it as too heavy on social theory (Calvin, 13).

Bantam let *The Female Man* go out of print in 1977 as genre fiction relied on a churn of the new, but a letter campaign by feminist bookstores encouraged the eventual 1978 reprint. (See Kristen Hogan, *The Feminist Bookstore Movement: Lesbian Antiracism and Feminist Accountability*, 2016, 51) and after that Bantam opted for licensing it. As the book spread it began to gain traction. In 1981 Douglas Barbour wrote for the *Toronto Star*: [It is] A work of frightening power, but it is also a work of great fictional subtlety ... it should appeal to all intelligent people who look for exciting ideation, crackling dialogue, provocative fictional games-playing in their reading'. Elizabeth Lynn, of the *San Francisco Review of Books*, described it as 'A stunning book, a work to be read with great respect. It's also screamingly funny' (Calvin, 2010).

Yet the book continues to puzzle and vex. In 1985 the Women's Press Book Club gave it a UK promotion when it became one of the first sf books in their monthly book selection. In that year, Laura Marcus wrote in *The Times Literary Supplement*,

> 'Joanna Russ has learned all that a radical feminist science fiction writer should know about the genre; but this does not prevent *The Female Man* from being very

nearly unreadable. Her prose is a singular affair, **marked by a simplicity of diction** and a remarkable obfuscation of temporality, context, place, addresser, addressee, and ultimately of the point.' (My bold: it does not seem to have occurred to Marcus that if an English Professor uses simple diction there might be a reason.)

In 1986 however, Tom Moylan in *Demand the Impossible* positioned *The Female Man* as a powerful literary montage (65) and deployment of Utopia as praxis (82).

The reception of *The Female Man* was (and is) complex and this is also true in the classroom. Catherine McClenahan in 1982 reported, 'When I have taught this novel, a typical series of reactions [from female students] goes like this: 'So far I don't like reading this book; I'm confused…I'm starting to enjoy it…it's venting some of my anger… I don't know whether to cry or yell… it's as if Russ has been bugging scenes from my own life' (McClenahan, 114). Ritch Calvin (2010), who also provides the best summary of contemporary reactions to the novel, was disappointed by the book's reception among his undergraduate classes (every student hated it), and later among his graduate students undertook to consider the book's initial reception. I had a similar experience and learned to hand out a Harlequin romance for students to use as a comparison. But the book remains in print.

By 2010 Gollancz was receiving a lot of push back over the almost entirely male masterworks list: selected only from books they already owned, it was an inevitable consequence of the buying policy under Malcolm Edwards, but in representing itself as a list of key texts was increasingly out of step. They asked for nominations of female authors and there was a great deal of support for *The Female Man*. There is no question that is now regarded as one of the classics of the field.

The Covers

The Female Man has regularly fallen out of print and been passed around publishing houses, and as it has moved, it has been recovered. These covers demonstrate the emerging respect for feminist science fiction, the growing esteem in which *The Female Man* has been held, and to some degree the mainstreaming of the novel.

The early covers are frankly terrible. The 1975 Bantam cover by Morgan Kane and the 1977 Star Press cover by Peter Elson, feature 'exotic' and frankly chilly women posing for their portraits. Then in 1978 Bantam replaced their cover with a sepia print of a woman, naked from the waist up, holding up a planet (possibly a reference to Mao Zedong's rallying cry, *women hold up half the sky*). That is the last of the truly terrible covers and also the last of the sf-mainstream covers until the twenty first century. *The Female Man* moved, for the next twenty years, into niche publishing and with that some much better covers. The Women's Press covered *The Female Man* with abstract art from Judith Clute (1985) which you will find on the cover of this book, two arms held up to form a portal into a pastoral scene; Beacon Press simply placed a white woman with her hands on her hips, against a lawn littered with shoes (Louise Sullivan, 1986) but then replaced it in 2000 with more abstract art (an eye looking through a circle) by Anastasia Vasilikis.

In the 1980s the book was translated into German (1979, naked woman with crown and trident, Wojtek Siudmak; 1980, naked woman in cream, by Poen de Wijs), into French (also Siudmak but this time two odd, fey creatures, half dalek and half semi naked floral fairies), and into Spanish (two covers, no dates, both with portraits intended to be half male and half female). Italy's is better: J. Bettag shows two women, both martial, one inside a portal the other outside, against a field.

In the 1990s things improve as the consensus settles on the abstract: Easton Press in the USA produced a really lovely green embossed cover of a woman emerging from a Women's Power symbol (1994, Clee Richeson), although in the UK the Women's Press replaced Clute's iconic cover with a rather generic profile of a woman à la Tamara de Lempicka, in blue and pink, by Amanda Ward (also 1994).

In 2000, Beacon Press, as noted above, go abstract; Goldstone Press opt for what looks like clip art (it's uncredited) of two naked and unspecified heads, back-to-back (2002); and the German edition opts for a fragmented page with various symbols of womanhood including lipstick which succeeds in being both abstract and representational. Then we have another gap until in 2010 when Gollancz finally included *The Female Man* in their Masterworks series with a purple cover showing three identical women holding hands around a spinning portal by Dominic Hartman. It is very effective. The book was re-covered in 2022 by Autun Purser, as part of Gollancz's return to their iconic yellow backs. Purser specialises in rather beautiful 1920s style travel posters of sf titles, and these four strips each fit his style; but the four yellow stripes of alternative worlds, while accurate and representational, do nothing to indicate the power of the book inside the cover. I'd tentatively suggest that there is a conscious attempt to avoid 'girl cooties' from the cover.

Looking at the covers there is a clear sense of the book moving from pulp, through marginal and then to classic, but only a few of the covers seem to engage with the power for the book: Judith Clute's, Clee Richeson's and the first of the Gollancz covers by Dominic Hartman.

Moving On...

Discussing the book's narrative strategies, as we will be doing here, is in some ways easier than summarising it. More than one critic has struggled to convey the plot. Janis Kelly, reviewing it in 1975, simply described each of the four worlds. LeFanu, fascinatingly, dissects it then summarises it, and then, frankly gets lost seconds after trying. 'The plot of *The Female Man* could cause quite a headache if mulled over too long. It is based on the science fictional premise of parallel probable worlds, but is subversive of the classic SF paradox of time-travel...' (189). This, gentle reader, is not a plot summary. Neither is the segue into the relationship of Whileaway to us. And when LeFanu concludes, 'The plot of *The Female Man* concludes...' with the choice offered by Jael, you can be forgiven to wondering if you blinked and missed something. But LeFanu does try. Cortiel skips over plot and decides to head straight into a deconstruction I have made much use of, but there is a feeling that for Cortiel the book is a manifesto not a novel. Mandelo suggest that this is a book without plot, or 'what could be labelled as a plot in mainstream critical discourse' (Mandelo 24): to

Mandelo this is a book as argument not a book as story, to which I will return in chapter 3, as I find this a useful way in which to understand the book.

Gwyneth Jones, who is a novelist, does recognise the book as a novel, with a story to tell of four women or a version of one woman who, 'pass in and out of each other's realities' (55), a description which has so much more movement in it than does Cortiel's approach. Jones, I think, also sees this far more as the character Joanna's story than do the other critics, with which I agree. Joanna, for all her passivity, has an agenda; she is on a quest to find possibility. Jones tackles the need to find story by taking us scene by scene through the book and there is a great deal of summary. But at the end Jones concludes,

> '*The Female Man* is Year Zero art: an anti-fiction, with all its fictive effects vivisected. There is only one character, the writer, deconstructed. There is only one story: how she came to embrace radical feminism while retaining a feminine past, still living inside her, whose alter-ego is a fury of repressed rage…' (68).

This is too metaphoric for me. I recognise what Jones is saying, but for me each of the four stories in this book— Joanna's about living in a female body while trying to compete in a male world, Janet's of homesteading, Jeannine's dreams of romantic escape and her real life 'romantic' ending, and Jael's search for an ally in a war—all combine to create a story, one that makes more sense when we remember that Russ liked ghost stories, and argued (for example) that we cannot understand Charlotte Perkins Gilman's *The Yellow Wallpaper* unless we understand it as part of the Gothic. *The Female Man* is a Gothic: Joanna is the character who calls up the ghosts, and each of the other characters are past, present, future (or futures), time-ghosts who let Joanna interact with her rage, they are real, however, not metaphor.

Perhaps the clearest is Angelika Bammer's description:

'The three women meet in the present (Joanna's time). But this is a present that opens on to a fourth dimension in which past, present, and possible future converge. Jael represents yet another dimension. Neither past, present, nor future, she cannot be defined in terms of either time or place: she embodies all possibilities. Her role is to remind the others (and implicitly us, for she is "the spirit of the author")... that not only do we shape the future of our present actions, but these actions are themselves shaped by our vision of what the future might be' (95).

Of the Js she argues 'What one of them is unable or willing to do, one of the others does for her' (102), thus Janet uses her martial arts to reject unwanted advances, Jael deploys the cartoon violence that Joanna fantasises about.

'Basic [Rough transition] to all three of these texts is the assumption that alternative worlds are not just abstract fantasies, but concrete possibilities that emerge as the material conditions and the consciousness of a society change... to become historically actualized requires active intervention...' (Bammer, 97).

It is Bammer I am probably closest to, but I am not convinced that Jael is the spirit of the author. I think that all of the Js are the spirit of the author, and that it is rather important to hold on to that (Jael's account of the discipline she experienced after she dismissed the 'girly' girls, is a lesson to the reader not to dismiss Jeannine).

Catherine McClenahan made a serious attempt to consider that *The Female Man* is best understood through its form, an approach that this book will also take. In her 1982 article on textual politics and the uses of the imagination, McClenahan argues that we need to understand *The Female Man* as Blake-style visionary art, not a novel or work, but a Barthes-ian *text*, 'an activity, a production, of both work and reader together'. This seems self-evident in the Brechtian style of *The Female Man* and the combination of direct address through the Greek Chorus and performative aspects, and in the way Whileaway is presented to us both through Janet's interviews and documentary-like as a travelogue. McClenahan identifies a trajectory within the text: A) A Choice of Evils; B) The World Re-Imagined; C) Liberating Anger and Desire and D) Uniting the Contraries (which could be mapped well on to both the Aristotelian ideas of Unities and John Clute's Grammar of Fantasy). Each of these sections uses different techniques to link the characters in different ways that McClenahan suggests give us polysemic meanings and trajectories for each character. These will be picked up in later chapters. McClenahan writes, 'Instead of packaging a meaning for us to get texts keep deferring a final or single meaning...In short, texts *play*.' (114)

All of the summaries and descriptions of *The Female Man* are all very different, but this is not because any of us have misread, but because this is a profoundly modernist and polysemic book. I suspect Russ would be disappointed if each of us had read the same book. We all interpret differently because of the sheer density of this book. What follows next is, I hope, a different way of considering it.

Chapter Three: Character

In this chapter I want to take up Stephanie Katz's idea that there is a reading experience in which the 'reader looks for connections between character identities rather than connections of plot events' (Katz, 148), and that the connections and disconnections are embedded in the rhetorical and stylistic choices that Russ makes for each character.

This section explores the four Js as characters, voices and subjectivities, how Russ 'voices' them, and the diegetic modes she chooses, so that each conveys not only through content but through style, who she is and where she fits into her world. I will be drawing on Dorrit Cohn's models of psycho-narration, quoted monologue and narrated monologue, which seem to *fit* better than diegetic models do.

In her essay, 'The Addressee Function, or the Uses of Narratological Laity…' Dwivedi argues that

> 'Not all subjectivities are constructed through techniques analogous to those of natural narratives. Not all require a speaking subject once focalization and the unspeakable sentences of free indirect discourse compose the narrative situation, nor does all focalization project an intentional stance' (2018, Ch. 13-e-copy).

We all see all of this in this chapter.

In Cortiel's article, 'Joanna Russ: *The Female Man*' (2005), Cortiel explores the quintet of Janet, Jeannine, Joanna, Jael and Joanna Russ as reflections or commentaries on their respective worlds, and as commentators on their worlds. Cortiel argues that 'The stories of women's agency created in her texts are not politically significant in and of themselves, but rather in how they strive to relate to the material existence of women outside the text' (17). In Cortiel's terms Janet is a replacement for the ethnographer of utopian fantasies, the traveller in the strange land. Becoming the confident explainer of her own society, Janet speaks as an insider, as the civilised being to the barbarian world; 'Janet represents hope and spiritual redemption, which corresponds to the undialectical Whileawayan version of history in which the men just died in a plague' (2005, 505). Jael 'references the painful and violent transition from powerlessness to agency' (2005, 504), she is the antithesis of Janet, angry and sardonic where Janet is calm and straightforward. Jeannine in Cortiel's construction is 'accordingly' the weakest of the four, the product of a society where women are pushed further to the margins and in which Jeannine was promised a fairy tale while denied education and agency. For Cortiel, Joanna seems least real: 'Joanna's textual world is steeped in ambiguity, indeterminacy and uncertainty driven by her imaginary interactions with Janet, Jael, and Jeannine, in all of whom she sees herself...' (2005, 506-508);

> 'everything, including her own transformation, takes place between her psyche and the act of narration... the novel is her therapeutic narration, and the other plot lines are her

own Utopian dreams, nightmares, or allegorical stories juxtaposed in a postmodern pastime of feminist vignettes that together constitute a scathing critique of the USA at the cultural moment of 1969' (2005, 507).

I do not agree with all of Cortiel's arguments here: there is an ethnographer in this text—the ectoplasmodiegetic[1] character of Joanna/Joanna Russ/the narrator—but it is an unreliable one, as is also Janet, the narrator of her own world; I am not convinced that Jeannine is not a narrator, her voice 'confined to the level of character speech— controlled by the narrative voice' (2005, 506); and I think Joanna is a far more integrated character, and far *more* of a character, than Cortiel's arguments suggest. I do not agree with Cortiel that there is no point at which the characters are ever integrated. Part IX is, for this reader, precisely the re-integration. And I very much don't agree that the stories of women's agency are not political in and of themselves: Russ the materialist feminist and labour activist, and later author of *On Strike Against God*, is viscerally aware of the importance of stories of agency in the movement. But overall, Cortiel's summaries are sensible and there is no real need for me to unpack them.

The book is split relatively evenly. Janet has twelve sections, Jeannine thirteen, Joanna fourteen and Jael nine. Jael does not fully take the stage until chapter VIII and there is some question over whether the ghost (fourteen sections) is Jael or Joanna, or Russ. Around forty sections

---

[1]. I am indebted to Paul di Filippo for this construction. I am fairly sure he was joking in response to a Facebook post about narratological terminology, but it's just too good not to use.

are heterodiegetic, with the omniscient third person often in observational or performative mode.

In his essay on the implied narrator, Wayne Booth argues, 'in every corner of our lives, whenever we speak or write, we imply a version of our character that we know is quite different from many other selves, that are exhibited in our flesh-and-blood world' (Booth, 2008, 77), a process he calls masking and unmasking. In *The Female Man*, Joanna Russ is engaged in rendering this process (self)-conscious, in brackets because she wants us to be conscious of it too.

Dorrit Cohn, moving away from the idea of diegesis which is solely about the manner in which something is told, offers three terms:

- **Psycho-narration**: a fusing of omniscient description and internal analysis; conventional description by an omniscient author without any attempt on the part of the author to disguise this; 'it is not primarily a method for presenting mental language' (12). [Joanna]
- **Quoted Monologue**: direct thought quotations (13), where the character describes his or her feelings aloud. This is essentially what we think of as Brechtian, a mode of monologue that is also a form of Discourse. [Janet]
- **Narrated Monologue**: 'He had of late—but wherefore he knew not—lost all his mirth': what we think of as stream of consciousness. [Jeannine]

With these tools in hand, let me begin to think about the characters, taking them in the order in which they appear.

Janet

Janet opens *The Female Man* (Part 1/I) with what initially seems to be the kind of internal monologue characteristic of first-person narration, but which gradually emerges, in tone and direction, as responses to a formal interview. 'I was born on a farm on Whileaway' concludes with a summary of her job (Safety Officer), her IQ and that of her wife, her cv and skills, and a summary of her family, and in sentence 10, a piece of explanation that renders it clear she is talking to a stranger: 'Since then I have been Safety Officer for the County, that is S&P (Safety and Peace)…'

The structure of the sentences of the lengthy paragraph (38 lines in the Women's Press edition, 18 sentences) is one I associate with the thriller: it begins long and complex and ends staccato.

Sentence 1 & 2: 'I was born on a farm on Whileaway. When I was five I was sent to a school on South Continent (like everybody else) and when I turned twelve I rejoined my family.'

Sentences 2-12 range from twelve to fifty-five words. 'But Yuki is crazy about ice cream. I love my daughter. I love my wife. I love my family (there are nineteen of us). I love my wife (Vittoria). I've fought four duels. I've killed four times.' Juxtaposed in those staccato sentences are the mundane, the intimate, and the brutal.

What do we learn of Janet in this opening? Janet takes herself for granted. She does not mean to shock. The cognitive estrangement of this paragraph is ours, not hers.

Janet reappears in sections III and IV and is the first indication that we are not in a linear timeline: it is Janet's first appearance in the chronology, though brief. The swap with the policeman is not instantaneous. Janet appears, the policeman disappears. Janet disappears, the policeman re-appears an hour later. Time (and distance) has passed. Janet remembers what has happened, even if she thinks it's someone "mucking about with my head!" (1/III). The section is told third-person omniscient, always referring to her in full as Janet Evason; it focuses on Janet's *response* and her character is depicted through that response. Janet doesn't scream, faint or act puzzled: she immediately drops into an evasive position and when tackled by a policeman begins to respond physically before he disappears. Janet is someone who *acts*. The final line of this section, 'But who has been mucking about with my head!' said Janet Evason, has a peculiar, dead pan comedic quality (aided perhaps by the replacement of a question mark with an exclamation mark, rendering the line graphic) that we will see repeatedly. Janet, the one not constrained by the expectation that men joke, women laugh, is funny.

In section 1/VII we see Janet interviewed on TV—Joanna and Jeannine are watching from a bar—and we see Janet through her responses to the assumptions behind the interview questions. Janet is bemused at the assumption that men are *significant*. Janet works through the Reason (not logic) being offered to her by the male interviewer. In a mode that undermines the interviewer, Janet responds with short, bemused and revealing statements.

> MC: …Surely you expect men from our society to visit Whileaway?
> JE: Why?

…
MC: Don't you want me to return to Whileaway, Miss Evason?
JE: Why?
…
MC: … Do you want to banish sex from Whileaway, Miss Evason?
JE: Huh?

Janet refuses to defend her world, because her world is complete. It is not, as the interview implies, lacking, and unlike so many guides to Utopia, it is not her own world she feels needs glossing. Janet, perhaps more than anyone else in this novel, is embedded in a fully-built world and as a result, if you asked Janet if she were cognitively estranged by her experience of Earth, she would probably laugh, because Janet has a sense of humour and to Janet, the behaviour of people on Earth is not estranging, it's objectively funny.

When Janet lands she is surrounded by military men. 'Three took out a small revolver, and this surprised me; for everyone knows that anger is most intense towards those you know… There's no sense, after all, in behaving that way towards a perfect stranger; where's the satisfaction?' (1/V).

But this is a continual doubling of *our* cognitive estrangement because Janet's narrative voice her quoted monologue, shapes our understanding. Our estrangement is positioned to see our world through Janet's eyes, and to see how strange our own world looks:

'a young woman walked in, a woman of thirty years or so elaborately painted and dressed. I know I should not have assumed anything, but one must work with what one has; and I assumed that her dress indicated a mother. That is, someone on vacation, someone with leisure, someone who is close to the information network and full of intellectual curiosity.'

The signs Janet reads send a completely different set of signals to the ones of our modern world so that Janet also confuses the men not only by her appearance but by her misprision and ideology. Janet arrives unarmed but aware of threat, the interviewer reproves her: 'An armed person is more formidable than one who is helpless. An armed person more readily inspires fear.' JE: Exactly.' (2/VII). Janet receives the lines from the men as feeders for her punchlines.

Part 3 1 & II which is also discussed in terms of Joanna, and focalised through Joanna does offer us some insight into Janet. It is easy to see Janet as a typical Whileawayan and thus representative, but we have already been told that she might not be. In these two sections, we see Janet's behaviour change from 'company manners' in which she listens to Joanna's chiding, 'civil, reserved, impenetrably formulaic' (3/I) to a reaction to 'the official tolerance of everything she did' (3/I) which leads her to abandon her own Whilewayan manners and push the limits of what she can do. We've seen this before. When in the TV interview Janet is asked how the women of Whileaway do their hair, her answer (*with a clamshell*) is a realisation and push back against Othering and Orientalism, and again, funny. The humour is delivered through point and counterpoint, observation and response.

We also see Janet (as she is narrated by the heterodiegetic Joanna) as knowledge hungry—absorbing newspapers, novels, data sets, textbooks etc; we see her 'neat but lazy' (3/I) and having fun with room service. Janet is (in)advertently portrayed as a curious mischievous child (or is it Joanna projecting the expectations of the barbarian this time?), and also as a young girl awaiting her come out. In Joanna's expectations, she is preparing to meet the man. Janet of course is doing nothing of the sort, and we watch her (3/II) approach the party at the Riverside apartment with dubious scepticism: *alcohol is a waste of grain, pretending you like something is an alien script*, and she does not understand why someone would be spending time with not-friends, people you don't like. The exchange between Janet and Ginger Moustache is a masterclass in non-communicative discourse as he tries to chat her up by talking about his wife and children and gives Janet the impression that he is a caregiver; and as he attempts to 'get to know her' while appearing right on, and Janet defies (refuses would imply that she understands what is happening) the script. When Janet explains about her duels, the most alien aspect is that for Janet a motive is not necessary, temper is an adequate explanation: Whileaway (and Janet) is not a society that disguises or excuses its behaviour.

The final conversation is with Ewing, the despiser of feminism. As Janet sits listening without expression (him: 'You're a good conversationalist'), Joanna kicking her under the table, and whispering/thinking various versions of *please don't hit him*, we realise Janet is increasingly out of patience. But note, out of patience, not angry. Even when she is at her loudest, shouting at him, Janet is in control: as he flips through the options in his metaphorical and actual blue book, she laughs, shrugs and slaps him. When he goes for her, she quickly gets him in a lock hold and when he refuses to believe what's happening, that lock hold breaks his arm. Janet is merely puzzled, '"But why do you want to fight when you do not know how?"' (3/II). The scene concludes with Janet, affectionately, telling Joanna to throw away the blue and pink books. To Janet, both are comical fictions.

In Part Four, with the exception of XVI, the Janet sections are ectoplasmadiegetic; the observations of the ghost (Joanna?). The ghost does not *describe* Janet, she constructs the space that Janet takes up so that although this chapter is ostensibly about Janet, it is to a far greater extent about the Janet-as-observed by the ghost, which is not quite the same thing. As we learn about Janet in this chapter, we also learn something about the ghost (and earlier about the interviewer), and the Janet we learn about is tinged with the ghost's anxieties and desires and taboos. In 4/I Janet stands in the bathroom and sings Handel's 'I Know that My Redeemer Liveth'. The narrator/ghost/Joanna interjects to note that Janet is singing *She*, when it is a man: 'But of course she doesn't listen' (4/I). Janet doesn't listen: to Janet there is rarely anything worth listening to. Janet does not *refuse* to listen, but the sounds that Joanna's world makes lacks semantic meaning (see 4/X, 'I know the language but not the context. I can't judge this').

The Janet that Russ creates is prosaic because she lives in a world where women do not need to hide their reactions: 7/IV is one of the sections in which we learn as much about Janet (who is being observed) as from Joanna, the intradiegetic narrator. Janet is following strange men; it bothers Joanna. Janet is explaining cultural customs, strange to us they are both blunt and transparent and oddly non-communal—if Whileawayans meet and both say 'no' they fight—a challenge to the 'utopia' of 'When it Changed'. Janet tells us of her job as a peace and security officer, a role she fills because she is *not* smart in Whileawayan terms: the exchanges with Elena Two, the attempts to get Elena to come home, are witty and sympathetic, but in the end, she shoots her. Whileawayan communitarianism is enforced, not consensual. Janet is blunt, and unsentimental not because she has no sentiment (she is profoundly romantic) but because Whileaway constructs sentiment differently. Janet finds metaphor both bemusing and hilarious for the same reason; and her humour is broad because no one has ever told her that her laughter is inappropriate, unfeminine or threatening to men. Nor has she ever feared that a man might kill her. Janet is ur-woman, woman outside of bi-gendered culture, a woman who cannot exist in our world. Not, in fact, a woman, but a person.

Jeannine

Jeannine sections are single, focalized and are written in what Franz K. Stanzel (1984) called 'a figural narrative', a third-person narrative in which the world is channelled through the eyes of the character, or through narrated monologue. Formalist and structuralist ideas of character, see characters as actants who perform certain actions and have no psychology; this works for many of the performative, staged set pieces in *The Female Man* but it also applies to Jeannine.

The narrative which characterises the Jeannine section is detailed in the extreme: Jeannine is Mrs Dalloway, her skin stripped and her thoughts on show but at the same time watched (focalized) by others, sometimes Joanna but sometimes others. Although this is a superficially third-person observational and heterodiegetic narrative, this is misleading: the interiority which characterises the Jeannine sections is one in which Jeannine *is* the heterodiegetic narrator, endlessly re-narrating her own life in an effort to land on the correct story.

> Jeannine Dadier (DADE-yer) worked as a librarian in New York City three days a week for the W.P.A. She worked at the Tompkins Square Branch in the Young Adult sections. She wondered sometimes if it was so lucky that Herr Shicklgruber had died in 1936 (the library had books about this).[2] (1/II)

This move from the external description of Jeannine's condition to an internal thought is a frequent trajectory in this introductory section. 'Jeannine balanced on one foot. (Nice girls don't do that.) She climbed down the ladder with her books and put them on the reserve table. Mrs. Alison didn't like W.P.A girls.' (P1/II)

The last line is not external but internal. It is Jeannine's reflection, not the narrative description. Jahn writes, 'the figural text appears to be determined by the filtering and coloring devices of the reflector's mind... the reader...

---

2. Joanna Russ was Jewish, giving this an extra layer of implication. Oddly, while there are many fantasies in which Hitler won, worlds in which he never existed or, as in this case, remained Herr Shicklgruber, are rarer: Stephen Fry's *Making History* (1996) and Jon Courtenay Grimwood's Alexandria trilogy (2001-2003) are examples. It also means that Jeannine's New York is a lot less Jewish than our New York.

becomes a witness rather than the narrator's communicative addressee' (Jahn 2007, 96). This is not Genette's disinterested non-focalization. This section, ostensibly externalised, and what Richardson in *Extreme Narration* (2006) calls the 'hypothetical form' (29), is actually drawing us in to her mind:

> The cat jumped off, knocking over one of her Japanese dolls. After dinner Jeannine took him out; then she washed the dishes and tried to mend some of her old clothing. She'd go over her ration books. When it got dark she'd turn on the radio for the evening program or she'd read, or maybe call up from the drugstore and find out about the boarding house in New Jersey, She might call her brother. She would certainly plant the orange seeds and water them. She thought of Mr. Frosty stalking a bath-robe tail among the miniature orange trees; he'd look like a tiger. If she could get empty cans at the government store (1/II).

Russ uses this swoop from the external to the internal to reflect the narrowness of Jeannine's life structured by poverty, limited aspirations, and the consequence lack of agency. The second half of this opening section doubles down, with an exchange between Jeannine and Cal (whom she dreads seeing) as she acquiesces to his determination that there will be sex that afternoon. The conclusion to the section emphasizes the two focalizations, external and internal, '"Oh, all right," said Jeannine hopelessly, "all right." *I'll watch the ailanthus tree*. (1/II)'

Where Janet is all confident internal coherence, Jeannine is fractured, incoherent, a muddle of incomplete internal thoughts many of which she cuts off because she doesn't want to hear herself express her misery over

Cal who she does not like and who cannot afford to treat her, the contained poverty of her life and the smallness of her dreams. The narrative of Jeannine is intimate and affectionate. It is perhaps because Jeannine is the weakest of the Js that her sections are the most intradiegetic (Janet's the most extradiegetic). Jeannine retreats into her head and into comfort, '(*I have my cat, I have my room. I have my hot plate and my window and the ailanthus tree*)' (1/II) and later into imagining her cat's activities in her absence.

Shulamith Firestone argued that romance was constructed in the 1920s precisely to control nascent feminism, so that it makes sense that it is Jeannine, in a world in which women in the US didn't join a demanding Second World War workforce, and that never saw the civil rights movements of the 1950s, who is mired in it. Jeannine has two types of dreams: those rooted in her tiny, constricted reality such as her pleasure in Mr Frosty's experience with a fish, and that of the faux romantic, cinematic dreams of being found by a well-off man who thinks her beautiful. Jeannine has the 'resolute focus on a single, developing relationship between heroine and hero' that Radway found characterised the most popular romances in her focus group (1984, 122). Both contrast sharply with the reality of her old coat and cheap make up. Jeannine's sections are constructed from floating details, a wisp here and a wisp there extending the duration of the sections in ways that reduce rather than enhance significance. Jeannine laughs to herself at the way the elderly lady on the bottom floor looks is a way to deflect her own fear. She doesn't look like *that* (1/X).

But within the novel, Jeannine's narrative and character trajectory will be outwards. In Part 2, Jeannine is the subject of Joanna's observations, the terrified passenger in the Cadillac 'gripping the car seat at my back (the way children do)' (3/III). In IX she is picked up (carrying a dual meaning) at the Chinese New Year Festival (for Madam Chiang, celebrating the recapture of Hong Kong from the Japanese, who in this world without a Second World War, hold the Chinese mainland). Jeannine, as we have already seen, has a repertoire of responses that she acts out both physically and in her head and here they construct a scene of terror and seduction: Janet whispers in her ears, she protests, she imagines refusing the invitation/kidnap with a swirl of beauty, ambition and self-possession, and in the end, as she does with Cal, nods, 'petrified' but also perhaps aware that she is living out the being swept off her feet that she has longed for and fantasised; and yet with enough of Joanna's acuity and Janet's practicality to register that the reason Janet's coat doesn't fit, is that it belong to one of the plainclothes policemen (2/IX).

If Jeannine's trajectory is outwards, first she needs to break her own cognitive script. Voicing it, as she does in 5/II to Joanna in the subway, is part of breaking it. The script is, like all cognitive scripts, self-supporting. Jeannine identifies why she is unhappy with Cal and then, having explored her (non or imaginary) options she circles around in an act of self-convincement both that Cal is 'sweet' and that she 'enjoys' being a girl.

In 6/I Jeannine wakes from a dream of Whileaway. She is preparing to spend a week with her brother and his family and her mother, at their summer home by the lake. She 'has' to go, she goes every year, it's both expected and resented by all involved. This sets the tone for what follows, what should be pleasure is pain, what should be a release from the cares of the world, brings on new cares. 'Everything's a cheat' is the driving message of the entire chapter. We follow Jeannine as she prepares for the vacation. The sentences accumulate, falling over themselves as chores fall over themselves, in a scene reminiscent of Pamela Zoline's 'The Heat Death of the Universe' (1967).

> 'Fill the pail, find the soap, give up, mop it anyway with just water. Put everything away. Do the breakfast dishes. She picks up a murder mystery and sits on the couch, riffling through it. Jump up, wash the table, pick up the salt that falls on the rug and brush it up with the whisk-broom. Is that all? No, mend Cal's clothes and her own. Oh, let them be [she doesn't]. She has to pack and make her own lunch and Cal's (although he's not going with her). That means things coming out of the icebox again and mopping the table again...' (6/I)

The sense is of chasing order, constructed from short internal instructions, and halted by the continual realisation of more to do. Whereas in the Zoline story, internal disorder is played out in external entropy, here the external constraint is projected onto housework and by extension onto Jeannine's sense of self.

Jeannine is truly only interrupted by the daydream scripts that insert themselves: the thought of a romantic love, how she would refuse him, she never refuses Cal; the thinking about what she has packed, the discouragement when her suitcase is too heavy because 'little things make Jeannine blue', the nostalgia of her teen years and wondering what it is other women have or know that she doesn't have or know.

Jeannine's inner monologue is one of *discomfort*, her self-narration about trying to fit herself in, to explain herself to herself, her self-justification of herself as a woman in a world in which there are both rules and script and also unknowns. She snaps the leash on Mr Frosty (the cat) and 'In a few minutes he'll forget that he's confined. He'll take the collar for granted and start daydreaming about sumptuous mice. *There was something unforgettable about her…*' (6/I). The segue makes the link for us. Jeannine is trapped by the cultural script she has accepted, she has accepted the leash she resents, moments after it is clipped on.

Delorey, talking of the challenge Woolf faced, notes: "Woman's sensibility has been constrained within those limits by the dutiful conventions of the heterosexual social fiction" (101), which seems peculiarly appropriate. and which she narrates to herself. The italics (representing this scripted daydream within the internal monologue) perform the same function Delorey identifies in Virginia Woolf's use of parentheses, they deflate and destabilise the 'traditional masculinist narratives' and continents, they open up a space for the '"moments of being" that had historically been seen as parenthetical to the real workings of the world'"

In 6/III we meet Jeannine's family and also learn a little about Jeannine. She was smart, she practiced talking and pressed wildflowers. Her relationship with her mother is one of passive aggression (her mother) and passive aggressive retreat (Jeannine). Mrs Dadier also has scripts: she cleans—she is giving her daughter in law a holiday, although she is staying in a separate cottage—arranges flowers and tries to arrange her daughter's life. In 6/IV Joanna (a ghost) joins Jeannine on the clubhouse porch. Here Joanna becomes the voice of cultural reason: they only want what's best for you; your mother is a wonderful woman; there are no good jobs, and anyway the men get them; marry someone who can take care of you; do you never want a home of your own? Joanna, as we know from 6/II is projecting. She is trying to turn Jeannine into the Joanna that Joanna herself resents.

Mrs Dadier comes in, but in that second, Janet appears and it is Janet who reacts, Janet who pushes Bro away, who threatens to knock his teeth in, who is in that moment the Ego, the person Jeannine and Joanna want to be. But it lasts only seconds, and Jeannine is back into her cringing apologia, apologising for being outside for wanting to see the moon, to have ambition: Bud, 'well, you've seen it… [we've] been talking about you and we all think that you've got to do something with your life. You can't just go on drifting like this. You're not twenty any more, you know.' Which of course will mean introducing her to a man. Any man. A second-hand man not yet detached from his wife. The chapter concludes, "Well, who shall I marry?" said Jeannine, trying to make it into a joke as they entered the building. He said, with complete seriousness: "Anybody".

6/V is The Great Happiness Contest. It slides directly in front of the scene we've just seen played out and continue to see played out by Mrs. Dadier and Eileen Dadier. This Brechtian performance is uncomfortably close to the defensive and declarative happiness of the 'the housewife', cramped and confined into a narrow definition of fulfilment. In 6/VI Jeannine prepares herself to perform it, 'Jeannine is going to put on her Mommy's shoes.' Jeannine is going to search for her Cinderella ending, she forces herself to date an unattractive married man, she sits in the movie theatre at the lake (6/VII) and falls in love with an actor, 'It didn't matter which actor or which character she fell in love with; even Jeannine knew that; it was the unreality of the scene onstage that made her long to be in it or on it or two dimensional, anything to quiet her unstable heart' (6/VI). But why is her heart unstable? Jeannine scours herself, engages in a Socratic dialogue with Joanna/the ghost:

> I said Jeannine, why are you unhappy?
> *I'm not unhappy?*
> You have everything (I said). What is there that you want and haven't got.
> *I want to die.*
> Did you want to be an airline pilot? Is that it? And they won't let you? Did you have a talent for mathematics, which they squelched? Did they refuse to let you be a truck driver? What is it?
> *I want to live.*
> I will leave you and your imaginary distresses (said I) and go converse with somebody who makes more sense: really, one would think you'd been balked of some vital necessity.
> …
> *I know.*
> …You can't expect romance to last your life long… (6/VII).

In this explication of the problem that cannot find a name, Russ, as is so often the case in this book, uses Joanna as the devil's advocate presenting Jeannine with the dilemmas she feels: that the only way a woman can want is to want to be exceptional, to want to be *ordinary*, and yet to still want more is to build 'a whole philosophy from the cry of the crickets' (6/VII)

In chapter 7/IV Jeannine almost disappears, 'she flattens like a film of oil; she vanishes dimly into a cupboard, putting her fingers into her ears.' When she finds a dildo, Joanna convinces her it is a communication device, that it will blow her mind, she 'will be lost to all respectability and decency and decorum and dependency' and all the things that crush Joanna/Jeannine and which are for Jeannine. Then she reappears at the start of 7/V: it is here that Jael /the ghost creeps down the stairs and 'observes' each in the kitchen. Each in turn monologues to the ghost, Jeannine doubles down, 'I try to make the right decisions...', digging into her unhappiness. Jeannine then more or less disappears until 9/VII where, in the very last scene in Schraft's, now disgusted at her own world, she is the only one who invites Jael in. Jeannine knows there is nothing she can do to change her life, but maybe Jael can. Jeannine's narrative trajectory is one that understands that liberal arguments about agency are distractions from the need for material (and materialist) change.

Joanna

When we first meet her, Joanna is our interlocutor, 'a disembodied voice that poses questions which the narrative goes on to answer' (Richardson, 2006, 79) and although she will resolve into an on-stage character, this construction is how this novel is both didactic and catechistic. At times Joanna's questions will be rhetorical, at times directed to the reader and at other times, as intra diegesis, to the character.

Dorrit Cohn argues for a mode she calls **psycho-narration**: a fusing of omniscient description and internal analysis into a narrating character. Crucially, 'it is not primarily a method for presenting mental language' (Cohn 12). Cohn's category assists with the difficulty of placing the character Joanna within the language of diegesis. Joanna is a homodiegetic first person narrator who thinks and comments within the story but who at the same time is a stand in at the for the author, may overlap with the ghost, and is just one element of the Book of Joanna in Part Nine. Joanna can see everything, but it is not all her story; as a character she makes use of Free Indirect Discourse, creating a sense of slippage between the narrator and the character-focalizer, offering an authoritative, but judgemental voice (Mezei 77) with the result that Joanna's sections frequently overlap or integrate with the Performative sections.

Joanna first appeared in 1/IV as the ghost-observer commenting on Janet's return to the New Forest. She reappears in 1/VII in a cocktail bar, watching Jeannine and also watching the television set. What the scene tells us of Jeannine and Janet I will consider in the section on interaction below, but here I am interested in what it tells us of Joanna.

Joanna watches Jeannine rather than the television set. She is an observer narrator of the world around her and through her we begin to pick up details of Jeannine's life. Joanna is as inclined as we all are to consider herself 'the norm' even while this book will in part be about her discomfort-in-the-world. In this section Joanna takes on the mantle of the neutral, scientific observer and compares the other characters mostly to each other, but not to herself.

Joanna the observer is in a constant state of defining herself through what she is not.

Thus, Joanna notes the 'Little woman child with the wee voice' on the tv advert trying to sell her something over a sink. She rejects her identification with this woman-construct. Joanna contrasts Jeannine's droopy femininity with Janet's besuited masculinity although she uses neither the word feminine nor the word masculine, a deliberate decision I think, and by doing so places herself between them. Joanna, it seems is a very precise person who notes and judges from details. This judging sits alongside Jeannine's whining and solipsistic criticism of the world, and Janet's tendency to recount her own world in facts. Joanna is analytic, Jeannine critical and Janet an uncritical ambassador for her world.

Part 2 is short (just eleven sections): and though introduced by the ghoul, Joanna and Janet dominate much of it. Joanna, in the key sections II, III and IV takes over the story and the narrative. It is in section II she 'turns into a man', and in which Joanna, 'living with' Janet's presence on the TV, also lives with a translucent semi-present Jeannine, striving to break through the looking-glass into Joanna's room, calling not for Joanna, but for Janet. It's the first hint that the three may be intimately connected.

Part 3, section I & II form around half of the entirety of Part 3 (9 pages of 18 in the Women's Press edition). 3/I begins,

> 'This is the lecture. If you don't like it, you can skip to the next chapter. Before Janet
>
>   arrived on this planet
> I was moody, ill-eat-ease unhappy and hard to be with.'

The layout clearly matters because it fragments the prose. My suggestion is that it is intended as a theatrical prologue. Imagine Joanna on the stage, she begins the monologue. As she finishes the third line, she steps to one side, and the curtains part. We see a girl (she uses the term 'Other girls', this is the young Joanna) brush her hair, dress, bat her eyelashes, practice defence, all told in short staccato lines:

dress for The Man
smile for the Man
talk wittily to the Man
flatter the Man
…
live for the Man

The entry of Janet, who Joanna conjectures she called from nothing or who called up her, disrupts this. But this Joanna is not yet ready to thrill to this disruption (except illicitly). Instead, Joanna positions herself as the teacher, the benevolent mentor, the chaperone. It is profoundly imperialist: Joanna frames herself as the civilizing influence 'I taught her how to use a bath-tub.' Joanna is in control of the Hollywood style transformation scene 'I took her out of her workingwoman's suit and murmured (as I soaped her hair) fragments of sentences that I could never finish 'Janet you must… Janet, we don't'. (3/I) Joanna 'put(s) shoes on that woman's feet; she watches her walk around naked and practice her yoga. Joanna puts lipstick on Janet and watches it disappear. She finds pictures of naked men for Janet, and a small baby boy to be examined. She submits to having her back scrubbed and being required to scrub in turn. Yet as the section goes on, Joanna loses control of both the narrative and of Janet. Janet laughs at girlie magazines, she plays games with Room Service, she finally dresses, 'a study in purest awe as she holds up to the light, one after the other, semi-transparent garments of nylon and lace, fairy webs, rose-coloured elastic puttees' and punctures Joanna's romantic imaginations by wrapping one of the elastic puttees around her head. (3/I). The romance ends in comedy, 'She bent down to kiss me, looking kind, looking perplexed, and I kicked her. That's when she put her fist through the wall.'

Does Joanna kick Janet because a woman has just tried to kiss her? Does Joanna kick Janet because this is the script between a Man and a Woman—approach, be repulsed, react with frustrated physical violence expressed in a form that shows physical restraint from hitting A Woman? Joanna's relationship to the script in this scene is constructed from her resentment and confusion and anger at her own confusion in the face of a world that feels wrong and a set of roles that fit as well as the panty-hose that Janet refused.

On to the next scene at the party when this sense that a script is being disrupted and dissected will intensify. Focalized entirely through Joanna, it begins with Joanna's focus on herself and then moves entirely to focus on Janet. Joanna, uncomfortable in dress, updo, make up, and feminine underwear of pantyhose and bra, projects onto Janet both the freedom she desires and the fear she has of that freedom. 'In we walked, Janet and I, the right and left hands of a bomb' (3/II). 'I shadowed Janet' (3/II) carries more weight than merely the social. In this scene, Joanna is

Janet's shadow, Janet is Joanna's projection. The analysis is Joanna's (the observation of The Chorus), the disruption is Janet's even as Joanna ostensibly seeks to control and shape Janet's behaviour.

This scene is classically portal fantasy: Janet is the world traveller and like all world travellers is dependent on the guide figure (Joanna) but here, unusually, it is focalized on the Guide (Joanna) rather than the Traveller (Janet). Joanna's tension and complex relationship to and fear of the scenario draws attention to how unreliable the Guide figure is. The Guide has her own agenda; a mix of desire for and resentment of conformity. Within this construction the Guide's outsiderness is both form and function: Joanna observes and critiques but does not challenge, because Guides (mostly) do not: Guides are a product and representative of the society they explain. When Janet is being harassed, we get the following (the italics indicate Joanna's unspoken thoughts).

> '"Let me go," said Janet.
> *Say it loud. Somebody will come rescue you.*
> *Can't I rescue myself?*
> *No.*
> *Why not?*
> All this time he was nuzzling her ear and I was showing my distaste by shrinking terrified into a corner, one eye on the party. Everyone seemed amused' (III/2).

Joanna, the Guide, watches as Janet breaks 'the rules'. Janet calls the man 'savage' and as Joanna—slipping into the Performative mode notes, ' he looked up "savage" only to find to marked with an affirmative: "Masculine, brute, virile, powerful, good"' (3/II). When the scene is over, the book the Male chorus carries flutters to the ground and Joanna picks it up, comparing the scripts for male behaviour with those for female behaviour in each respectively.

> 'They do fit together so well, you know. I said to Janet.
> "I don't think you are going to be happy here." [Joanna to Janet]
> "Throw them both away, love," she answered.'

The Guided takes over the Guide position. The Guide, relieved, acquiesces.

Joanna is both a Guide to Janet on Earth, and to the reader on Whileaway. The descriptions of Whileaway are postcards, snapshots of a place she can only observe (3/IV to XII) and add a melancholy to the construction of Joanna's frustration and rage.

If Joanna positions herself to guide Janet to a feminity she herself resents and resists, Joanna sees Jeannine as her weaker self. Part 5/I opens with Joanna, stuck with Jeannine: she is sitting in a subway car observing and listening to Jeannine fuss with her hair, with her clothing, with her life. Joanna turns it inward. Noting Jeannine's fussy clothes—loose and shapeless, raglan sleeves, overflowing and oversized—allows Joanna to think about the clothing of her own youth, tight, repressive, containing; boned, cinched, high-heeled, with much extra material (double circled skirts instantly dates her), coats with no buttons, brooches that caught. Both Jeannine and Joanna are caught in clothing that makes movement hard. But it is the self-consciousness that

I find interesting here: Jeannine's is a self-consciousness entirely culture-bound, a form of vanity in which she both hopes for, and fears being, looked at. Joanna's is the doubled self-consciousness in which she is aware of both the self-consciousness of being female and she is self-conscious of that self-consciousness. This drives 5/II in which Jeannine dialogues with an essentially silent Joanna who is aware of how the dialogue is supposed to go but is opting out.

What most puzzles Joanna (6/IV) is how she got stuck with Jeannine. But is Jeannine her own id? The instinctive or acculturated impulses that she has resisted? In one of the Jeannine episodes, Joanna slides into the room. In 6/IV Joanna has been watching Jeannine and narrating back to her the script she ought to be following, that Joanna too should be following. The constraint or imprisonment self-imposed by both Jeannine and Joanna is a continual thread in the book. Much of what is constructed as feminine is self-constructed to avoid a fight. Joanna's awareness leads to anger, but the anger is directed inwards. In 6/II Joanna rages that she dresses and makes up, flirts, does things for others (especially men), but, a single line, 'I'm frigid.' She excoriates herself, she is angry, despairing, a slut, contentious, disorganised, 'But O how I relish my victuals! And O how I fuck!' This is about dualism and living between that dualism.

Part 7 is the part that has stuck most in people's minds, because it is one long shriek of pain and rage from Joanna, and here it is that shriek I'll comment on. It begins, famously, 'I'll tell you how I turned into a man. First I had to turn into a woman (7/I).

Told as a long continuous prose poem, Joanna dissects for herself and us the process of becoming one of the boys, the enforced self-invisibility, the abdication of femaleness, the betrayal of that identification and the constant sense that true acceptance/maleness is just around the corner, 'when I had acquired my PhD and my professorship and my tennis medal and my engineer's contract and my ten thousand a year and my full-time housekeeper' (7/I). And had acquired the mentality that allows the comment she has a man's mind to pass as a compliment. Joanna is undercover. She can show Janet how to become 'a woman' because it is a performance. Like Anne Bannon, the writer of pulp lesbian romance, Joanna

> 'always felt like a visitor from another planet, successfully disguised as a young girl. It became a sort of game; I would dress, talk, gesture, and move like other little girls, but I would keep the secret that I was different somehow and didn't really belong in their company.' (email exchange between Abate and Bannon, 2004, 175).

This stream of consciousness thought has been predominantly Jeannine's up until now; I think Russ is using it here to bring the two characters together. Jeannine has turned her rage into depression; Joanna has turned it into inner despair and self-hatred. Jeannine has become the consumptive heroine, fading away; Joanna is the Baba Yaga (or a repressed Jael). Both fundamentally feel uncomfortable in their world (Janet and Jael do not). We can contrast two pieces.

Jeannine 6/I	Joanna 7/I
She hauls at the valise again, wondering what it is that other women know and can do that she doesn't know or can't do, women in the street, women in the magazines, the ads, married women.... [Jeannine] knows that men—in spite of everything—have no contact with or understanding of the insides of things. ...who is to use all this loveliness, who is to recognize it, make it public, make it available?	I'm a sick woman, a madwoman, a ball-breaker, a man-eater; I don't consume men gracefully with my fire-like red hair or my poisoned kiss; I crack their joints with these filthy ghoul's claws and standing on one foot like a de-clawed cat, rake at your feeble efforts to save yourselves with my taloned hinder-feet; my matted hair, my filthy skin, my big flat plaques of green bloody teeth...

In these two quotes we have that difference, Jeannine begins self-critical, Joanna begins analytic; Jeannine ends in bafflement, Joanna in rage. Both characters partake of the gothic, Jeannine as the innocent but doomed heroine, Joanna as the grotesque and monstrous corrupt.

Joanna looks around and sees no women: King Kong is male, the Devil is male, the man who dropped a bomb on Hiroshima is male. 'I was never on the moon' (7/I). Sociobiology classes are delivered in such a way that the male is active, the female passive. Joanna gives a long list of all the things done by men, said by men, defined by men, but things are better now and notes that 'New Yorkers (female) have had the right to abortion for almost a year now if you can satisfy the hospital nears that you deserve bed-room and don't mind the nurses calling you Baby Killer' (7/I).

> 'Anyway every-boy (sorry) everybody knows that what women have done that is really important is to constitute a great, cheap labor force that you can zip in when you're

at war and zip out again afterwards but to Be Mothers, to form the coming generation, to give birth to them, to nurse them, to mop floors for them, to love them, cook for them, clean for them, change their diapers, pick up after them, and mainly sacrifice for them. This is the most important job in the world. That's why they don't pay you for it' (7/I).

Rage tumbles over itself, the phrases falling into entropy and those final two short capstone sentences.

Joanna herself critiques this mode: 'I have no structure (she thought), my thoughts seep out shapelessly like menstrual fluid, it is all very female and deep and full of essences, it is very primitive and full "and's," it is called "run on sentences"' (7/I). She has become Jeannine. And yet, as we will see with Jael, the I, the self-narration, is not without power: Joanne S. Frye wrote, that for women writers to 'speak directly in a personal voice is to deny the exclusive right of male authority implicit in a public voice and to escape the expression of dominant ideologies upon which the omniscient narrator depends' (51, cited Richardson 2006, 74). Thus, perhaps the assumption of the first person is a generative and political moment.

Most of what we learn about Joanna is that she is *enraged* and that rage is made up of thousands of small slights, and sheer envy of the innocence of [white] men, and that she is conscious of living in a world in which Man encompasses and claims space, that she can demand *only* if she becomes a man.

Part 9 is both a summing up and a reveal. It opens with a statement, 'This is the Book of Joanna.' In Judaism, the Books are the Megillot, the stories of people rather than the people. Is Joanna here Samuel the prophet? Esther the brave? Ruth the loyal? There is a lesson here. In part 9, Joanna becomes all the characters: Jeannine constantly put down, Janet who loves Laura, but Joanna who is frightened by that attraction, Jeannine and Joanna who have grown up in a man's world, and Jael who will slam a door on a man's thumb (9/V).

In 9/VI Joanna traces the process by which the small Joanna, a scientist in the crib, who 'thought very well of myself' is pressed into 'Joanna', whose illusions about the world in which her mother is President, are dispersed. But here, at last, Joanna begins to find herself, meeting a real Laur (not Janet's Laur) and taking that key step, expressing the wanting and the asking and the acceptance, and then the embarrassment and the working out if it counts.

The book concludes with the meeting in Schraft's (9/VII) and as three of them leave, Joanna is left to say goodbye to the other three in her head, in one of the most lyrical sections.

> 'Goodbye to Alice Reasoner, who says tragedy makes her sick... who says die if you must but loop your own intestines around the neck of your strangling enemy... Goodbye to Janet, whom we don't believe in and whom we deride but who is in secret our savior from utter despair.... who comes from the place where the labia of sky and horizon kiss each other...Goodbye, Jeannine, goodbye, poor soul, poor girl, poor as-I-once was' (9/VII).

But are we saying good-bye to external or internal characters? Cortiel thinks the former, I think that here there is a merging, not into Joanna per se, but of all four characters into Joanna Russ. Mezei argues that 'by employing a polyphony of voices, Virginia Woolf paradoxically effaces the narrator, who is seemingly diminished by the presence of so many other (internalized) voices, yet she also enormously augments the narrator's structural role as he/she weaves from one voice to the next in a display of virtuosity' (Mezei, 'Who is Speaking Here' 8).

Russ takes up this idea and uses it at the end of the novel to bring herself, the narrator, the 'real' Joanna Russ, centre-stage as a Brechtian orator. The book ends, with the Voice of Russ.

Remember: we will all be changed. In a moment, in a twinkling of an eye, we will all be free. I swear it on my own head. I swear it on my ten fingers. We will be ourselves. Until then I am silent; I can no more. I am God's typewriter and the ribbon is typed out.
Go, little book...

Jael

Jael is, naturally, the hardest to pin down: in 8/I she is the ghoul in the elevator, the ectoplasm, the psycho-narrator, who wants to scare and to chill; from 9/1-VIII she is narrated by Joanna, from IX to XV in first person. In both cases the narrative is intradiegetic. The switch from one to the other mode is dramatic.

Is it Jael we meet in 2/I? We can't yet know. Printed in italics this opening is threat, and horror. This is the monster in the human skin 'skinny as a beanpole underneath' and a 'very impressive face' the ghoul (as she describes herself—

did the first readers assume it was a she?) rises up through the elevator and haunts it with a finger to the back of the neck of the rider. J4, the ghoul, Jael, has a sense of humour. Again, I am not sure if it is Jael we meet in 5/VI. But this narrator describes the arrival of Janet, Jeannine and Joanna on Whileaway. Also 5/XI is this Jael who is the guest of Vittoria? In this section a child (through Vittoria) tells Jael a fairy tale which is actually about the visitor. And the visit itself is cast into doubt as real in XVII. Why?

The whole of Chapter 8 belongs to Jael. In this chapter the ghost comes out of the closet, explaining to the three Js what is going on (although she is an unreliable narrator, so who knows). Jael is witty, self-deprecating yet vain, loves to show off and shock, enjoys and is bored by her interactions with man-land, and is in it for the war. Her mission is to engage the other three Js in the war in her time/place.

In 8/II Jael is described by Joanna who enjoys Jael's enjoyment of her enjoyment of the cliched speech; she steps forward, defined by her grey hair, lined face and 'rather macabre' grin. Joanna sees that Jael loves them, smiles like a goddess making Jeannine and Joanna at least feel loved—Janet is conspicuously untouched by Jael. She is Alice Reasoner, or Alice Jael, she has a soft, cultivated laugh, she also has a real laugh that 'is the worst human sound I have ever heard: a hard screeching yell that ends in gaps and rusty sobbing' (9/III). In 9/V Jael explains what is going on. She, Jael, is gathering together Js from different universes with the intention of planting bases on each Earth, she comments on each of the Js, noting the ways they differ but are expressions of the same genotype—there is no inevitability in Jael's world. In 8/VI Joanna notes that Jael is whispering into Jeannine's ear, seducing her in a scene that plays to Jeannine's fantasies, while Janet forces Jael into explaining the War, a war between Us and Them, between progress and reaction, between haves and have nots, between men and women. In 8/VII Jael takes them topside to see not the land of women that she comes from, but to Manland, where Jael acts as their guide to the risks, dangers, and the construction of Manland and to meet a Manland Boss where, in VIII we flip into first person.

In first person we discover that Jael has inordinate patience. Like Joanna she can wait out the bluster, the mansplaining and the silliness. Until she can't. But even then she is in control, enjoying herself, repeating a line from Joanna in part 8. "Take your filthy hands off me," I say clearly, enjoying his enjoyment of my enjoyment of his enjoyment of that cliche (8/VIII).

And enjoying the moment when he begins to threaten to rape her, 'the mode is a wee bit over familiar. I told him to open his eyes, that I didn't want to kill him with his eyes shut' (8/VIII) and pulls back the baggy skin around her nails to reveal talons and tears him apart. Jael revels in the 'intimacies of hate', 'raked him gaily', and scores under his ear and leaves him to bleed out on the carpet and notes that 'No business done today. God damn, but once they get that way there's no doing business with them; you have to kill them anyway, might as well have fun' (8/VIII), and then the contemplation of what she could have done instead, what her colleagues, might have suggested, one of the Js asking whether it was necessary (probably not Janet) and Jael's response: "I don't give a damn whether it was necessary or not... I liked it" (8/VIII). The character of Jael is simultaneously attractive and repellent. Perhaps attractive because repellent? Jael is an opportunity to explore Wayne C. Booth's concern in *A Rhetoric of Fiction* that a sufficiently persuasive impersonal narration, and the very act of following the internal consciousness of the character, is potentially polluting of the reader's moral character. Jael, like Joanna, perceives herself as an external narrator in control of (if not the plot) the other characters. This tendency to regard herself as the controller to the narrative is a flaw she shares with the Boss man who is her alter ego in Manland.

8/IX shifts mode. As they fly back to Jael's residence, Jael becomes contemplative. We find out about her life in the refugee camps, about learning the essential lesson that feminine women (woman-women) are not lesser, and about being sent as an envoy to another culture posing as a male, experiencing male bellicosity, and insecurity and humour around that insecurity; a story in itself, and the way in which 'Hate is a material like any other' is embedded in the personality of this lively, charming woman. Jael is the extreme of Joanna and the antithesis of the calm and logical Janet; but both of them kill people. But if 9/IX matches Jael to Janet, 9/X—Jael's nightmare—matches her to Joanna. 9/X is a performative analysis of rape; rape as a Christian mystery, rape as revealing the dirt in a woman's soul, the awareness that 'cunts were all right if they are neutralised one by one, by being hooked on to a man' but how even this is not enough; how men complain and women are restrained, and how Jael decides that she does not want to restrain, and that she murders 'because I was guilty'. The chapter ends with a list of all the things 'you' (men) want from women and worst, require them to be happy at the same time.

The nightmare over, Jael seeks solace with Davy. When she is discovered (9/XI-XV) she explains what he is. Quite literally the object(ification) of sex. Connected to the house, empty of all but the weakest volition, having explained this to the J's she sets out her plans. Sex is invigorating for Jael, sex is extracted from human relationships, sex is materialistic not spiritual.

The Four Js

Russ's multiple focalizations, her narrating and narrated Js, appear to be a literary experiment with the masking and unmasking argued for by Booth in which the masks each get the chance to meet each other, and in which the masking and unmasking of the Implied Narrator becomes the Story (though not the plot). Russ uses Bakhtin's notion of intersubjectivity—the presence of several different narratives from which the narrative must be assembled—to construct the connections between character identities which Katz argues can drive a story, and what Attebery calls distributed selfhood (2022, 16) and which he argues is part of a mythic tradition. Before Jael arrives, Janet, Jeannine and Janet function as a triple goddess.

There aren't a huge number of scenes in which all three appear together. In the first, 1/VII, Joanna goes to the same cocktail bar Jeannine finds herself in, having appeared in Joanna's world, and both watch Janet on TV. The interaction between Joanna and Jeannine is short, but it is noticeable that Joanna in this moment is outside the story, she knows that Jeannine is from a timeline where the Depression hasn't ended and 'Fashion (it seems) is recovering very leisurely.'

In 5/VII Jeannine, Janet and Joanna arrive on Whileaway: this section is written as play script. Joanna is invisible—is she the scribe? Jeannine starts challenging why they have not been met. But she does not question the discourtesy, but why they are not being treated as a threat and as a threat within specific parameters that assumes they are the invaders and the Whilewayans are vulnerable. Jeannine and Janet, each operating as two sides of the triangle of character, engage in a Socratic dialogue, with Janet each time repelling the argument that seems Reasonable with the Evidence that it is not. Jeannine is the vector for cold-war thinking, and Janet for pacifist anarchism. Jeannine creates story, Janet heads off each narrative. Jeannine's expression is full of buts, and suppositions, Janet's is extrapolative and evidentiary.

In 9/VII they meet in Schrafft's, a women's place—a chain restaurant linked to the Boston candy firm, where the food is 'dainty' (a 1964 menu lists asparagus on toast, cheese soufflé, creamed shrimp as entrées) where men aren't welcome (and although there is chicken on the menu there is no steak). They munch in silence (like Whileawayans). Janet hates the food; Jael loves it. Jeannine and Joanna say nothing. Jeannine throws her world to the wolves (or Jael); Janet, who has already made it clear that Whileaway can defend itself, declines. Jael tells her that her world created the plague that cleared men from Whileaway; Janet, who has figured that Jael is an unreliable narrator responds "No...I don't believe.' Joanna and Jeannine 'stared accusingly'.

In that moment, although Joanna believes each one of them is Everywoman, Janet—in Wittig's terms—is not a woman, she is not part of the alliance of womanhood against manhood because in her world there are only people. Janet weeps for Jael, or perhaps for all of them; Jeannine for the first time is happy; Joanna is typed out, but Joanna is also typed in, she has become one of Kristeva's narrators (1980, 74). 'The writer is thus the subject of narration transformed by his [sic] having included himself within the narrative system: he [sic] is neither nothingness nor anybody, but the possibility of permutation.. From story to discourse and from discourse to story' (Kristeva, 1980, 74). But Joanna, she, does not 'become an anonymity, an absence, a blank space'. Joanna is the structure, the pulling together of all five Js at the end of this narrative—Janet, Jeannine, Joanna, Jael, and in the end, *Joanna Russ*—in Kristeva's terms permitting the narrative to exist.

Chapter Four: The Structure of *The Female Man*

This chapter is about the way *The Female Man* is told, the way that the voice(s) of the narrative enact a story of their own. Once critics have noted that the narrative of *The Female Man* is fractured, and multi-vocal (but not, interestingly, polysemic) they tend to move along fairly quickly. *The Female Man* is clearly an experimental novel but what that experimentalism looks like is overwhelmed by the political force of the message. In this chapter I intend to break down the novel into its sections, and think about how those sections function.

In *Demand the Impossible* Tom Moylan describes *The Female Man* as 'literary montage' (83) constructed from different rhetorics and genres, and full of allusions. Paul March-Russell describes it as having

> 'a collage structure—its abrupt and often inexplicable juxtapositions of inserts, sketches, interior monologue anecdote, fairy-tale, diatribe, essay, and metafiction—not only disturbs the logicality associated with phallocentric thought but also reveals the extent to which another discourse, unbounded by patriarchy, has been rendered impossible' (179).

My only objection to this is the use of the term 'inexplicable'. *The Female Man* is very clearly a stream of consciousness novel in which the cohesive interiority has been fractured by the demands of living in a world which demands pretence. Even while the novel is, in its story narrative, almost aggressively linear, it is also in Stephanie Katz's terms (in her 2022 thesis), a spiralling circular narrative, in which timelines cross and recross, holding together non-linear interventions of *mise-en-scène* and observational moments. Yet although the *story* drives forward, it still is an example of Genette's anachronous narrative, told backwards (prolepsis), forwards (analepsis), and from side to side, with interjections of Observations and Performative Scenes.

The Female Man is a fractured novel. It is told in sections, sometimes seemingly unrelated, some lengthy, some very short. If there is any classical novel it resembles, it is Lawrence Sterne's *Tristram Shandy*: it meanders, it circles back, it digresses, at times it seems to be avoiding the topic altogether, and yet, like *Tristram Shandy*, it constructs a whole that is larger than its parts.

The Female Man is constructed of some very clear modes, or rhetorics, which I have called here Story, Performance, Observation (or sometimes expository), and Mise-en-Scène. At times, it looks more like a dramatic performance than it does a novel (and it is surprising it has never been either dramatised or even turned into an Audio book). Russ's narrators—Joanna, Jael, and Russ herself in many of the performative Scenes (see below) engage in what Lanser has, in *Fictions of Authority*, dubbed *extra-presentational acts*, reflections, judgments, generalizations about the world "beyond" the fiction, direct addresses to the narratee, comments on the narrative process all of which ensure that *The Female Man* while an entertaining novel is also analysis, critique and manifesto.

The division of the parts into sections varies considerably both in terms of the number of sections and thus their length, and the rhetorical choices made for these sections, and thus the overall pace. The four modes listed in the previous paragraph are not used equally, nor are they distributed evenly. Nor are they anything other than what I see. I would expect every reader to find other divisions.

- Story, those sections that move the story on, form the bulk of the novel (43 sections). Parts 1, 4 and 8 are heaviest on Story. This the framework for the other rhetorics: Story holds the performative, the observational, and the Scenes; the Story sections are hypo-diegetic, short stories about each character, embedded within the larger narrative which is, unusually, extra-diegetic and is constructed through the hypo-diegetic Observations and Scenes.
- Performance, the short sketches in which archetypal interactions are replayed (26 sections). Performance scenes, which have a thematic function (Rimmon-Kennan 93) are relatively evenly distributed but there are more in parts 4 and 5 which are also the two longest sections.
- Observational or anthropological sections are those in which we are told something about whichever world we are in (31 sections). The Observational sections have an explicative function (Rimmon-Kennan 93), operate to investigate and outline the worlds we are in and function as guide.
- The *mise-en-scènes* are the snapshots, short glimpses of another world. Another critic might of course

divide these differently, or even with these terms come up with a different count. In each of the following sections I will explore the different forms, their rhetoric and how they sit in the novel as a whole.

Story

There are four stories in *The Female Man*; Joanna's, Janet's, Jeannine's and Jael's, and there is also one story, the story of their interaction. This section is more about structure than it is about style or rhetoric because much of the discussion of story style can be found in chapter 3, character.

The interaction of the monologues, and the observations, the performances, and the short scenes, drives the stories.

All four stories are structured as biographies into which enters change.

Joanna's story, which she retells, is of her life as a woman in a man's world, of the need to become first neuter, then a man, and then the *disruption* to this model caused by the arrival of Janet, who is neither man nor woman but *a person*.

Jeannine's story is a romance: the story of a woman who must decide between her 'career' and 'the man who loves her' in the context of a precarious job, an unsympathetic but normal family, and a strong hint that Jeannine's interest in women is purely theoretical and romantic in the sense of an internal generic narrative.

Janet's story is that of the explorer, who has an affair with the native, knowing she will return home to her loved ones.

Jael is searching for a place to site the equivalent of an aircraft carrier.

The forked narratives which allow for each of these stories is a not uncommon one in science fiction but here the narratives cross and recross. Chatman argues 'If we were to extract randomly from cocktail chapter a set of events that happened at different times and different places to different person, we would clearly not have a narrative (unless we insisted on inferring one…)' (Chatman 1978, 21). That is precisely what Russ constructs and demands we infer the story from; each of the stories told matters. Russ constructs not one voice or four (or five) but all of these and a communal voice, 'a collective voice or a collective of voices that share narrative authority' (Lanser 21).

This is a multiply framed Story. Richardson argues that, 'frames are in fact inherently unstable. They invite their own deconstruction because they appear so definitive yet are obviously partially arbitrary and capable of being reconstructed or placed themselves within a larger, different frame' (330). In *The Female Man* it is tempting to construct a hierarchy in which Joanna's story is the frame for Jeannine and Janet but as later, Jael becomes (she insists) the frame, and Janet suggests that perhaps her world is the driving actor in the plot and not Jael's, the temptation should probably be resisted. Russ's argument perhaps is that we all think of ourselves as the frames for everyone else's story, challenging whether the frames in this book are even real, whether there is an inside or outside, and whether the frame is a place in itself.

The Female Man opens with Story: 1/I is Janet's autobiographical direct narrative (which we later learn is delivered to interrogators); 1/II is indirect narration of Jeannine Dadier's day; 1/III recounts in the third person what happens when Janet Evason appears on Broadway in her underwear, and her sleepy return to bed, bed partner and dream; and 1/IV introduces Joanna, sitting in a cocktail party and who has, in one of the most memorable constructions of the book, 'changed into a man... I mean a female man of course.'

I don't think it is coincidence that each of these pieces is told very differently: 1st POV reportage by Janet; 3rd stream of observation but very intimate with the character and following Jeannne on a movie dolly; 3rd proscenium-arch narrative in which Janet is subject not object; and the final piece in first faux authorial voice that I think I want to recast as first-person critical voice. Perspective on the world is one of the things that the story will carry in this novel. The narrative positions reflect the characters' comfort with themselves: Janet reports on her world, Jeannine is reported on and Joanna sees herself as set apart from hers, critic of it rather than author: Joanna as critic becomes Joanna the weaver of story.

This is extended to 1/VII. Joanna becomes the dominant narrative voice. These stories are overwhelmingly 'told' by the ghost version of Joanna: Joanna the observer, Joanna the narrator, so that even when they are not in first person—'Six months ago at the Chinese New Year, Jeannine had stood in the cold, holding her mittens over her ears to keep out the awful sound of fire crackers' (1/XII)—or they are the reported speech of one of the other characters—'JE: Evason is not "son" but "daughter". This is your translation.' (1/XV)—are still told from the point of view of Joanna. She is telling this story.

Joanna watches Jeannine and Janet from the cocktail lounge, positioning herself as a neutral reporter but in that position estranging us from what is reported, rendering the taken for granted, artificial. She contextualises the interview with Janet in 'our' wider world of twee adverts with 'little women' showing off an oven or sink advised by white-coated men; on the formal rituals of our world in which the handshake becomes an alien ritual absurdity, and in which the interview Janet gives—in her characteristically bald style—is rendered satirical, a deliberate (rather than accidental) comment on our world and its sexisms. This works because Joanna the narrator stories it, creating a doubled level of estrangement: ours of the whole, hers from her own world as she watches Janet puncture the verities.

The Jeannine sections carry the passivity of femininity, the Cinderella stories, the fairy tales in which the princess sits and waits: 'Jeannine dawdles' (1/X). In this section the most proactive thing Jeannine does is to feed the cat (Mr Frosty). The tenor or mood of these story sections is always languorous. Jeannine barely carries any story at all, and when she does finally take action it's in the wrong direction, towards an acceptance of Jael's story and argument. Where Janet is the centre of Janet's story. Jeannine's story barely has any Jeannine in at all she is both focussed on and resentful of others' stories, dreading being pulled into them, but always acquiescing. Jeannine shrinks from attempts to pull her into the core story, to bring her in from the periphery. We see it in 1/XII when Jeannine watches a Chinese New Year Dance, but holds her hands over her ears 'to keep out the awful sound of firecrackers' while in 1/XIII Janet stands in a parade in her honour and directs security guards to bring in Joanna. Jeannine's story always shows her to one side of Janet. Jeannine's is always passive verbs, Janet's active. In

1/XIV Jeannine, now on a farm in Whileaway, covers her ears and shuts her eyes and recites to herself '*I'm not here*'; the world overawes her, her narratives are always narratives of retreat. This is continued in 2/III when Janet Evason beckons Joanna into a stolen car and drives them all into the countryside: Janet is all action, Jeannine grips the seat and closes her eyes, and Joanna prepares to explain herself and, in 2/IV, asks , in one of the throwaway lines that punctuate the story sections, 'Was she trying to run away? Or only to pick people at rando?" In 2/V Janet explains.

Janet's explanation is storified. She recounts the choice of herself as traveller (she can be spared), being strapped in, and then appearing on the desk of the military officer. There is something about Janet's mode of travel and her appearances in 'our' world that reminds me strongly of *La Jetée* and although this story is all in first POV it is highly cinematic. Janet takes us through her movements while explaining as voice over what her thoughts were at any given moment, so that her thoughts, unlike Jeannine's random eructations, are considered and construct the surprise of the traveller in the strange land. One line in particular stood out to me: Janet 'held out the cat's cradle. It's not only the universal symbol of peace, but a pretty good game too' (2/V), because so many early sf novels assume that *something* will be the universal language, whether mathematics (even though that assumes common bases, and frankly, any foreigner who has tried to take the GRE will tell you that Americans do math differently) or humour (a story by Murray Leinster assumed all species would tell dirty jokes). Janet's story sections reliably work to undermine the assumptions of reader and destabilise our perspective on the world. The next section, although I have not included it in Story because it uses the observational mode, sees the scene from the other side in a report/ interrogation of the officer, in which an interviewer questions why Janet brought no weapons (2/VIII). This story picks up the estrangement: the core assumption that what a visitor should do is inspire fear, is a shadowing of the war that Alice Jael Reasoner is fighting. The story is beginning to unfold in these moments.

Part 4 begins with four story vignettes: in 4/I, Janet singing in the bathroom, of God the redeemer, swapping out the neutral he for the neutral she, Joanna asserting 'he's a man', and Janet, not listening; in 4/II, the family, told by the ghost who might be Joanna or Alice Jael; in 4/III, a description of Laura; in 4/IV, the poodle and the relief of the family, '"At least she's White," they all said.' Packed into these four short pieces is a lot of information and a lot of story: they tell us where Joanna is politically, and the short story of Janet's picaresque disruption of others' lives. 4/VII is the I that sits on the porch to look at the lights of the town? Who is the I who looks at the houses where children have played? It's not the I who is Janet who turns to Laur 'never thinking she might be lied to' who asks Laur if she likes living there. The section continues the focal move of the story to Laura, changes the focalisation while not changing the POV, which is essentially Joanna's. In 4/X, Joanna, floating on the ceiling, observes the interaction between Janet and Laura. Laura, swinging between 13 and 17 years of age, Janet sitting there, hall listening, speculating on Laura's attractions in a way that both Joanna and Janet regard as lewd, but *differently* lewd.

Part 6 is almost entirely story, but it is structured throughout as a play of resistance and acceptance. In part 6, Jeannine prepares to go on vacation, cleaning the house, mending Cal's things (of which more in a moment); arrives at the vacation cottage she shares with her mother; sees her brother, sister-in-law and niblings, goes out on a date with a man (the son of one of her mother's friends) and finally, at the very end, calls Cal, and asks him to bring her home, tells him she will marry him, and then splits, into the giddy potential bride that she needs to play, and the other Jeannine, the one that feels this is the end of her life, that she has accepted, not just second best, but a dead end.

The first section is told in dream fashion, following Jeannine around the house, as she undertakes the tasks she needs to do while feeling that there is something she has lost, that 'Everything's a cheat' (6/I). Life is a cheat: her orange juice is orange and grapefruit juice from a powdered mix provided by the government. She is not married to Cal yet she is trying to please him with clean windows, making his sandwiches, mending his socks. She wants to decorate, but the room is not worth decorating. The piece moves back and forward from Jeannine's decisions to her resentments in a see-saw motion which pushes forward, then pulls back, Jeannine's internal commentary always preventing both anger and action. When she collars Mr Frosty and thinks 'In a few minutes he'll forget he's confined' Jeannine sums up the mechanism of her own acceptance: minutes after each attempt to resent, argue or break free, she falls back into acceptance.

Later, in 6/III, we are told of Jeannine's childhood. A romantic child, one who sat in trees, whose first sentence was 'See the moon', who pressed flowers. Her interaction with her mother is one of pretence on both sides. Both smile only when others are present. Both lie to each other—Jeannine that she is no longer seeing Cal, her mother that she is happy and content. Jeannine lies to herself about her brother; he acknowledges her but does not reciprocate her adoration. In 6/IV Joanna enters the picture, but this Joanna is an antagonist, telling it like it is: *your mother is a wonderful woman, you will never get a good job, there are no good jobs, marry Cal*. Jeannine resists. It is as if Jeannine can only be resistant, on her own there is not enough drive. Then, just for a moment, Jeannine is traded for Janet, a woman who is not used to being told what to do, to being pulled around by a man, but Jeannine returns, and this time it's Bro who is telling her she should be married, she shouldn't be drifting, who reminds her, with a nasty joke, that spinsters are mocked and despised. Bro models for her what the world will look like for single Jeannine. When she asks, hoping that he will have a magic solution, who she should marry, the answer is 'Anybody'. The point is not that Jeannine be happy, it is that she should follow the script.

Calling Cal is to be the culmination of the story and everyone's dreams. Jeannine will tell her mother she's marrying him. Jeannine imagines how Bro will react. She thinks about how her mother will act when she announces a baby. Cal retreats from the story. This isn't about marrying Cal, this is about taking her place in the play that is life. Jeannine is all sparkle, all joy and in the background, on the stage, Joanna puts her arm around the other Jeannine, 'the shadow of her dead self… (who is desperately tired and

knows there is no freedom for her this side of the grave.)'
'And there, but for the grace of God, go I' (6/1X). Jeannine cannot reject, cannot rage, because there is no *traction* for her rage.

We go back to Janet in part 7/IV. Janet who, unlike Jeannine, is thoroughly in control of her own story. Janet is following strange men in the street, observing how they move and walk, how they greet each other. In defiance of Schopenhauer's idea that 'it is the inner life which is the true object of interest' (cited in Cohn, 186), Janet's story however is always told from the exterior, by Johanna or the Ghost. Joanna/Ghost tells us about how Whileaways greet each other. If they both say 'No', Janet says, they fight. It is a deliberate irony that the two insecure characters (Joanna and Jeannine) are told with interiority (Jeannine's sections are not strictly first person), which may hint at the insecurity of Jael in defiance of her defiance.

Part 8 is entirely story, and with the exception of 8/II is focalised on and mostly by Jael.

Jael. *Who am I?* (8/I).

Jael the ghost, Jael the ghoul, built of fake skin, fake teeth, fake (clawed) fingers. A cyborg built to scare the children

Section VI returns the point of view to Joanna but the narrative to Jael and this is the section that is most conventional in its story structure. Part 8 is the story of Jael who is in some ways what Joanna wants to be, the anti-Janet, the bringer of chaos. Where Jeannine dreams the frustration of her past, and Joanna is a muddle of anger, Jael's is cold, direct and clear. Jael explains The War, the divisions into like-minded communities of Traditionalists,

Neo Feudalists, etc (a list Gwyneth Jones picks up in *White Queen*), the war between Us and Them, Haves and Have Nots, eventually between men and women, the last ultimate divide. And all the time, Jael is targeting Jeannine. In 8/VIII it shifts again to Jael's POV: the story that Jael narrates is one in which we learn through contained observation. That observation is shaped by what Jael wants to show us, rather different to the more fly on the world approach of Janet's section). Jael wants the Js and us to be angry, so we are shown provocations. When the Boss man begins to perform some of the moves we have seen in the Performative Sections Jael keeps up an internal monologue combined with short—ignored—interventions; when he finally demands sex, Jael gets bored and moves into the dramatic 'OPEN YOUR EYES!' I roared, 'BEFORE I KILL YOU!', and his obligatory protests, *You led me on; you're a prude; you deceived me; you are a Bad Lady*. His story, however, is out of his control.

Jael reveals herself, her opening body described in detail, her killing scene, described like something from *A Clockwork Orange*, as something beautiful and skilled, the Js huddling in a corner, Jael laughing with both hysteria and joy. One of the Js questioning the necessity, Jael responding, 'I don't give a damn whether it was necessary or not… I liked it.' Jael's control of the narrative is total. The others huddle visibly but also rhetorically, their voices temporarily silenced by this woman acting in ways they all three associate with men.

Jael takes the Js home, and we get the description of where she lives (a palace) and tells them about the world she grew up in, as a traditional girl, and then a refugee, and then happy to be brought up a 'man-woman' until she told a teacher who let a 'girl-girl' beat the crap out of her. Jael tells of her espionage, of her role as an ambassador on a patriarchal planet, disguised as a man (in heavy clothing that hid everything), seducing a male retainer, taking a wife and discovering what it was like to be slavishly adored, but never hurting a Womanlander. Jael dreams of suppression and oppression, of a world in which women's role is whatever men want it to be but with the addition that 'On top of it all, you sincerely require me to be happy; you are naively puzzled that I should be so wretched.'

So Jael moves on quickly to her negotiation with the Js for bases on their world, Janet as an ambassador, Joanna and Jeannine because they will do. This is not quite the end of the story. In part 9, after Joanna has reprised the performative contemplation of her life as a revolutionary act, 9/VII returns to Jeannine. Jeannine is saying goodbye to her past life, she is Getting Married. The Js meet in Schrafft's (a famous place for women to have lunch, because it was genteel and cheap), its menu a story in itself about femininity. Jael is there to do business. Jeannine accepts. Janet declines. There is no recorded response from Joanna. The story ends, Joanna watches them go but stays also to merge with Jael and Jeannine and Janet, to show Janet the city.

The story, previously so clear, falls away, and becomes once more rhetorical, the goodbyes ritualised and cinematic, the typewriter falling silent, and finally the ending, a monologue, looking into the future, a something else piece of writing.

Performance

> This book is written in blood.
> Is it written entirely in blood?
> No, some of it is written in tears.
> Are the good and years all mine?
> Yes, they have been in the past. But the future is a different matter. As the bear swore in Pogo after having endured a pot shoved on her head, being turned upside down while still in the pot, a discussion about her edibility....she then swore a mighty oath on the ashes of her fore mothers (I. e. her forebears)....
> OH, SOMEBODY ASIDES ME IS GONNA RUE THIS HERE PARTICULAR DAY. (5/X)

Before she wrote novels, Joanna Russ was a playwright. When I was reading for this book, I was frequently struck by how easy it would be to stage it, and wondered why no one ever had. As we visualise this section, we can imagine groups of women in masks, stepping forward to declaim, the lone Joanna sitting to one side of the stage to deliver her monologues of commentary.

The performative aspects of *The Female Man* are the sections most often cited. They are a relatively small element of the text in terms of words but form around a quarter of the sections. Brechtian and humorous, as with the intervention with which I have begun this section, they are the segments that stop us in our tracks to laugh with bitter irony at ourselves, our worlds, and at the ways in which women are complicit in our own oppression.

Our first introduction to what I have taken to calling *the Greek Chorus* is in part 3, section II. Joanna has taken

Janet to a party. She feels uncomfortable: her bra, pantyhose (tights in the UK), bra, ring, all feel uncomfortable. Joanna is in drag. Janet, also primped femme for the party, appears comfortable. They walk in to find women who Joanna knows, to each of whom she has given a Greek-genre-romance nominatively determinative name:

> 'Spoisissa, three times divorced; Eglantissa, who thinks only of clothes; Aphrodissa, who cannot keep her eyes open because of her false eyelashes; Clarissa, who will commit suicide; Lucrissa, whose strained forehead shows that she's making more money than her husband; Wallisa, engaged in a game of 'ain't-it-awful' with Lamentissa; Travailissa, who usually works, but who is now sitting very still on the couch so her smile will not spoil; and naughty Sacharissa, who is playing a round of His Little Girl across the bar with the host' (3/II).

The women are reduced to masks because that is what the game of womanhood (as later outlined in the pink book) demands. Women's behaviour is constrained by the requirement to choose one of these roles. But the use of these caricatures allows Russ to critique head on what might otherwise be read straight. Russ' humour is not the humour of satire, it's the humour of Drag, the inflation of a situation to the point of Absurdity.

Once in place the playlets can begin. First with a round of His Little Girl.

> SACHARISSA: I'm your little girl.
> HOST: (wheedling): Are you really?

SACHARISSA: (complacent); Yes I am,
HOST: Then you have to be stupid, too.

This is one we all recognise, the woman who appeals to men through her youth and 'innocence' and keeps on doing it long past her youth (Sacharissa, we have been told, is forty-five). It's a game that assumed that what men want in a woman is an inferior, which is later played out in a scene of what we now (thanks to Rebecca Solnit) have named *mansplaining*.[1] On one level this scene is not funny, it's enraging. Its humour is bitter. Russ returns to it in 5/IX when she remembers a college freshman explaining her field to her at a party. She flips it.

EIGHTEEN-YEAR-OLD GIRL AT A PARTY: Men don't understand machinery. The gizmo goes on the whatsis and the rataplan makes contact with the four-thette in at least seventy percent of all cases.
THIRTY-FIVE-YEAR-OLD MALE PROFESSOR OF ENGINEERING (awed): Gee. (5/IX)

But still in 2/II, in A SIMULTANEOUS ROUND OF 'AINT IT AWFUL' in which LAMENTISSA complains that 'he' never notices domestic tasks, and WAILISSA first exhorts her to do better, and then collapses on her admission that no matter how beautiful her floor her husband *still* never notices. '(There follows a chorus which gives the game its

---

[1]. My favourite personal experience was the 'nice young man' who explained to me that I wouldn't want to be a 'token female' on the all-male panel on science fiction in which one man clearly knew nothing. I give my male companions credit for explaining to him exactly how he'd just made a total fool of himself.

name)' and a passing male who remarks '"You women are lucky you don't have go out to work."'

The anger here, however, is directed not so much at the man, taking women for granted, as towards the women who have projected their emotional wellbeing on to house work (as we also see with Mrs Dadier, Jeannine's mother, and Jeannine to a degree) and on to their husband's validation of that work in a world that tells them both that husbands appreciate it *and* that their role is to make domestic work invisible. The short scene is far more effective than the paragraph I have written to unpack it, because the chorus is instantly recognisable as a spiral that many women get into.

This act (2/II) is punctuated by these performances. Joanna is showing Janet Earthling behaviour: A MANUFACTURER OF CARS FROM LEEDS flirts by declaring that he has heard of American feminism and surely it's unnecessary. The Greek Chorus rush in with their 'Oh no, no, no!' Ginger Moustache tries to flirt with Janet by being a Right On Cool Liberal Man, giving her the cues she is supposed to recognise. Janet fails to recognise any of them so her *deadpan* responses, in which she shows off her duelling scars, project a humour so many of us would like to turn against such behaviour.

By the time the man from Leeds returns, Janet is seeing the game and begins to play it with both a vicious irony and an even more vicious straight line. Ewing, a colleague of Joanna's, tries to flirt with Janet through his intellectual superiority, then through the classic gambit of telling her *she's not like those other women*, nor is she an *extremist*. Janet tries to leave, but the host tries to grab a kiss and when Janet refuses he calls her a prude and grabs her by the wrist.

'Let go,——,' said Janet (some Russian word I didn't catch).
'Ha ha, make me,' said the host, squeezing her wrist and puckering up his lips...'

So Janet does. Janet does two things. She *goes loud*, breaking the rules for women drawing attention to the incident. She *takes it seriously* instead of laughing it off, again breaking the rules. Janet challenges the humour of the oppressor, the *just a joke* dynamic. Russ's humour understands that if we are to have a humour of our own, we must perform it. Janet yells 'Savages!' and her assailant reaches for his 'little book of rejoinders', but Janet has flipped things. Savage is linked to masculinity; he can't find it as a critical term. He tries again and she dumps him on his back. He is still flipping through his little book which he drops. Joanna picks it up. Its contents anticipate *The Rules*, they tell him what to do and how a woman will respond. Joanna takes out her own pink book 'for we all carry them'. Everything in her book is about *managing the man*.

But managing the man is never enough. In 5/IX we see the dominance game called I Must Impress This Woman. There is nothing funny about this one. As Joanna notes, 'I'm never impressed—no woman ever is—it's just a cue that you like me and I'm supposed to like that. If you really like me, maybe I can get you to stop.'

> SHE: Then if it's just a game and you like me, you can stop playing. Please stop.
> HE: No.
> SHE: Then I won't play.
> HE: Bitch! You want to destroy me. I'll show you. (He

plays harder.)
SHE: All right. I'm impressed.
HE: You really are sweet and responsive after all. You've kept your femininity. You're not one of those hysterical feminist bitches who wants to be a man and have a penis, You're a woman.
SHE: Yes. She kills herself.

Because the point is not for the man to impress but for him to (op)press. In order for this to work, however, women have to be complicit in their own oppression. And thus The Great Happiness Contest (6/V) in which each woman steps forward to list their blessings. The Great Happiness Contest is constructed as an accumulative competition in which each woman strives to be more blessed within the confines of approved ambition. This kind of accumulative game is familiar to children (You have x, he has x and y, I have x, y and z) but is also a mode of oppression Olympics, so that coded behind statements such as 'we have three darling children, each nicer than the last'—which uses a fairy-tale rhetoric in which the youngest is always the best and brightest or kindest—is misery and resentment released when 'ME' declares:

ME: You miserable nits, I have a Nobel Peace Prize, fourteen published novels, six lovers ... [etc]
ALL THE WOMEN: Kill, kill, kill, kill, kill, kill.

These performative moments are about showing the reader that their experiences are part of what we would now call a cognitive script, in which seemingly free will is channelled by expectations so rigid that acting outside them (six children is *too many*) or trying to break them is to confront a 'play'. But that these scripts are tying all of us. Mrs Dadier's and Bud's pressure on Jeannine to get married, to marry *anyone* is not about Jeannine, it's about maintaining the Game, of which the manuals are the blue and pink books.

> 'Men succeed. Women get married.
> Men fail. Women get married.
> Men start wars. Women get married.
> Men stop them. Women get married' (6/VIII).

> The merry-go-round cannot be halted by one of us unless it is broken by all of us.

A second type of performance is this book is the monologue. These are rather different from the interiority that Jeannine uses. Jeannine is addressing herself (see 5/II where, although in theory she is addressing Joanna, Joanna isn't listening and Jeannine asks only for rhetorical affirmation), the monologues dress the audience. When Laura monologues about being a victim of penis envy, and the problem of being a girl (4/I), she is addressing Janet (who isn't listening, but we are). The piece has the classic structure that Russ uses for these monologues of a long paragraph which begins with a small issue and compiles additional material to make the case. They feel as if they are checking off a long list of accumulated injuries:

> 'They say: of course you'll get a Ph.D. and then sacrifice it to have babies. They say: if you don't, you're the one who'll have two jobs and you can make a go of it if you're

exceptional, which very few women are, *and if you find an understanding man…*' (4/XI) The sentences run on. Even when they are relatively short; 'Boys don't like smart girls. Boys don't like aggressive girls. Unless they want to sit in the girls' laps that is. I' never met a man who wanted to make it with a female Genghis Khan' (4/XI).

The two major monologues are in part 7 and part 9. They are the two sections of the book where I think Joanna and Russ are genuinely conflated and deliberately so. Part 9 is discussed in its own chapter, Epilogue, but part 7/I begins 'I'll tell you how I turned into a man/First I had to turn into a woman' (7/1). This performance piece is about the performativity of gender (and precedes Judith Butler's 1990 *Gender Trouble* by two decades).[2] It begins with Joanna/Russ stating her position as a neuter. 'Not a woman at all, but One of the Boys', seeking acceptance through what the British call blokeyness and Trump infamously described as locker-room talk (*Washington Post*, October 7th 2016). And at each stage there is a feeling that the next man-achievement will bring acceptance. All selfhood is left at home. Any stepping into womanhood (the purchase of John Stuart Mill's *The Subjection of Women*) brings instant demotion once more to womanhood: 'to be female is to be mirror and honeypot', to be *nothing real* but what men imagine you, until you vanish at 45.

---

2. Interestingly, Butler is also from a Jewish radical family, although a generation younger. It raises the question whether the performativity involved in assimilation which fed into Russ's work (clearly acknowledged in both her fiction and non-fiction as discussed in chapter 1), and specifically the rather different demands of Jewish and American femininity, was also a factor in Butler's awareness of gender performativity.

In three paragraphs Joanna/Russ works through Greek dreams of being an oak tree, of Jewish prophets, of recognising oneself in someone impossible; then into the new liberties of Being a Woman, from New York's limited permissions for abortion, to the right to get cancer from cigarettes, to... being dead.

The monologue shifts between registers continually, from a list of behaviours, through anguished howl, self-reprimand and self-chastisement: a list of all the things the self said to force conformity leads into this beautiful rant comprised of received insults:

> I'm a sick woman, a madwoman, a ball-breaker, a man-eater; I don't consume men gracefully with my fire-like red hair or my poisoned kiss; I crack their joints with these filthy ghoul's claws... (7/I).

But even the ghoul, in an all-male world, is male. Even Grendel's mother 'was actuated by maternal love' (a trope male screen writers just *will not drop*). 'Whoever saw women *scaring* anybody?' Russ asks, dismissing the possibility that any of the Greats could have been a woman. Women's purpose, after all, is to be producers of the next generation, even at their own expense. 'This is the most important job in the world. That's why they don't pay you for it.'[3] And then she cries, and then she stops crying. For it is pointless. And so too is denial. 'I am a woman. I am a woman with a woman's sickness. I am a woman with the

---

3. In Lois McMaster Bujold's *Ethan of Athos* (1986), an all-male culture does pay for child-rearing. It costs a fortune. I suspect Bujold used the insurance figures for 'replacing' the work of a dead mother.

wraps off, bald as an adder, God help me and you' (7/I).

And at the end of all this? (7/II)

Well, I turned into a man.

There isn't space to go all the way through 7/II but it is, as Joanna says, 'slower and less dramatic'. We are given a litany of the natural world seen entirely as females-done-to and males-doing and yet, all of this rests on white male *trust*, as Russ segues into thinking about the degree to which all that is white-male-supremacist rests of enormous amounts of work being done by those supporting them, regarding their conversations and concerns as trivia. And then, unexpectedly, Russ segues into an experience of electroshock therapy described in the classic sf rhetoric of the sublime, the technological and the spiritual entwining in which the electrical wires become your own wires, and you become 'a conduit for holy terror and the ecstasy of hell' and the only solution to this is to love yourself because no one else will.

And thence to 7/III a lengthy list of male explanations for not listening: *not ladylike, shrill, limited.... trivial topics...* a list of the things that Russ expects to be said about *The Female Man* (and almost without exception were); the broken phrases indicating the distractible mind of women and the distracted mind of men when forced to listen to them. Concluding with a by now classic Russ mic-drop.

Q.E.D. Quod erat demonstrandum. It has been proved.

The three monologues in part 7 lead to this point. Whether you try to be a neuter, or a man, or a woman, you will always be A Woman, and thus not worth listening to.

Mise-en-scène

Mise-en-scène and Observation are very closely connected. By the former I mean the tableaux that Russ constructs and by the second those scenes which are almost anthropological—almost all (but not entirely) of Whileaway, they aim to show us ways of living.

Many of these are of course world-building, but they are notable because Russ breaks the 'rules' of modern science fiction and avoids all subtlety, while writing with great poetry. Two examples in part 1 are the first man on Whileaway (1/V), and our first full introduction to Whileaway (I/VIII).

> 'The first man to set foot on Whileaway appeared in a field of turnips on North Continent. He was wearing a blue suit like a hiker's and a blue cap.... The country's repair shed for farm machinery was nearby that week, so the tractor-driver led him there; he was not saying anything intelligible. He saw a translucent dome, the surface undulating gently.' (1/V)

This is the classic rhetoric of science fiction in which the mundane is used to set up the estrangement that catapults us somewhere else. Russ uses a dual vision, so that the man 'found them very odd: smooth faced, smooth skinned, too small and too plump, their coveralls heavy in the seat...' The tractor-driver, equally estranged, notes to the others, '"That, *mes infants*," said the tractor-driver at last, "is a man"'. One estrangement left open, the other closed with realisation.

In part 1 section VIII is inserted a lengthy piece beginning with an exclamation from Dunyasha Bernadetteson of Whileaway, 'Humanity is unnatural!' and which segues from a discussion of her jaw-line, to the perfection of her daughter's teeth, the plague which came to Whileaway and wiped out the men, in a world in which geological conditions had changed so much that 'natural conditions presented considerably less difficulty than they might have' a millennium or so earlier' (1/VIII). This section is almost classic world-building. It tells us about the way houses are heated, transport-networks function and how ova are merged; that intelligence is now controllable; and that the invention of the induction helmet transformed work. But that with all the industrialisation on Whileaway, there are no true cities, the planet uses its industry to maintain a pastoral culture (one which is clearly intended to emulate the *pastoral* of classical utopia such as *News from Nowhere*, while simultaneously defying it), and people still walk. This continues later with another lengthy piece of info-dump beginning with, 'On Whileaway they have a saying: When the mother and child are separated they both howl, the child because it is separated from the mother, the mother because she has to go back to work (3/IV). The six pages of text describing the rearing of children and young adults on Whileaway are direct: describing the activities of *they*... conscripted into the workforce at seventeen.

> They lay pipe (again, by induction).
> They fix machinery.

> They are not allowed to have anything to do with malfunctions or break downs… (3/VI).

The young people become adults at twenty-two and begin careers, sex and family. They dream of old age when they will recapture the liberties of youth. They are not monogamous and they work only three hours a day. Except they do not, because, 'there is too under it all, at the highly incredible explosive energy, the gaiety of high intelligence, the obliquities of wit, the cast of mind that makes industrial areas into gardens…' and a landscape of glider preserves, 'comic nude statuary' and all the many other qualities of utopia'. Because 'Whileawayans work all the time. They work. And they work. *And they work.*'

The lengthy info dumps are contrasted with poetic interventions, the tableaux which illustrate the info dump,

> A troop of girls contemplating three silver hoops welded to a little silver cube are laughing so hard that some have fallen down into the autumn leaves and are holding their stomachs…. (3/VIII)…

> Between shifts in the quarry in Newland, Henla Anaisson sings, her only audience her one fellow worker (3/IX)…

We learn as much from these brief interjections and we did from the lengthy description: where the latter tells us about Whileaway, the former gives us a feel for it. Some of the mise-en-scènes are very short. 3/XII consists of:

> Whileaway is engaged in the reorganisation of industry consequent to the discovery of the induction principle. Whileawayan work-week is sixteen hours.

The Mise-en-Scènes are the photographic snapshots, primarily of Whileaway, seen as if through a window. They are simultaneously the most neutral sections and yet also the strongest argument thread in the books. They are a presentation of a possible truth. Along with the Story sections they are actional: 'they advance the action of the first narrative by the sheer fact of being narrated' (Rimmon-Kennan 93). They are often the very shortest sections taking up as little as one line, but rarely more than ten, in which we are shown a swift scene, or given a free-standing one-line throwaway (10).

Observation

Observational or anthropological sections are those in which we are told something about whichever world we are in. The Observational sections have an explicative function (Rimmon-Kennan 93), they operate to investigate and outline the worlds we are in and function as guide. There are observational scenes in which Russ *explains things*. I could have included these in the monologues, but they lack their anger and drive.

> Sometimes you bend down to tie your shoe, and then you either tie your shoe or you don't you either straighten up instantly, or maybe you don't. Every choice begets two worlds of possibility that is, one in which you do and one in which you don't… (I/VI)

This begins a lengthy paragraph that explains alternative world theory but does so as a set of pictures which concludes by setting up what you need to know: that to the time traveller the present may belong to a past other than your own, that the future even more so, and that Whileaway 'is the name for Earth ten centuries from now but is not the future of *our* Earth' (1/VI).

But most of the observational sections are more mundane. Part 4 is almost entirely of this nature. It begins with Janet positioning herself as an anthropologist, moving to live with an ordinary American family, of father, mother and one daughter, Laura Rose Wilding (the name may be a reference to the author of that classic American figment of the literary imagination, *The Little House on the Prairie*).[4] The POV stays with the narrator and turns into an observation of the town and of Laura. In 4/X the narrator observes both Janet's and Laura's dreams, and how each reacts to them: Laura with hostility, Janet with amusement. Laura is threatened by her dreams. The section observes and records and *explains* the interaction between the two women: Laura proffering her reading matter (first magazines then mathematics) to Janet for approval, Janet reacting to Laura with respect, even when Laura goes into a defensive monologue which seeks to both hold off disapproval of the kind she is used to (for being an intelligent girl) and hold off Janet to whom she knows she is attracted. But I am less interested here in what happens than in how it is written. The hard proscenium arch with the third-person narrator is not sealed because the

---

4. Much of the *Little House* Books has been discredited (particularly the notion of the settler surviving without community help) but this was since Russ's day. I have assumed that she smelled a rat.

narrator, I/Joanna/Russ is right there, both in the room and as Laura so that when Janet kisses Laura and then takes her on to her lap the narrative is punctuated with commentary:

> 'Janet pulled her up onto her lap—Janet's lap—as if she had been a baby; *everyone knows* that if you start them young they'll be perverted forever and *everyone knows* that nothing in the world is worse than making love to someone a generation younger than yourself' (4/XIII).

The section contains two taboos, one ours—lesbian sex—the other Whileaway's—sex across generational lines, and the observation is reinforced by Janet's monologue as she explains why it is Bad but why she is going ahead. We segue to the bedroom and sex, and then, after a short intervention, to Janet's memoirs in 4/XVI-XVIII. XVI is about Janet's first experience of romantic love—a crush on her best friend, which crashed and burned and later turned into a longer lasting companionate love; XVII her time in a small town called Wounded Knee (is this our Wounded Knee? It's not clear) and her experience of *three-quarters dignity*, a time when young people are sent on a form of national service to work wherever they are needed, and to make connections across the planet; in XVIII we have an evaluation of the planet:

> 'There's no being *out too late* in Whileaway, or *up too early, or on the wrong part of town,* or *unescorted.* You cannot fall out of the kinship web and become sexual prey for strangers, for there is no prey and there are no strangers—the web is worldwide' (4/XVIII).

These three sections are each written with three variants of point of view: XVI is first person, Janet; XVII is first person the declared author, something relatively rare as the narrative voice usually identifies as the ghost or as Joanna; and XVIII written as straightforward commentary. The three of them fit together, the shift between the three voices working as a camera pulling back from the close-up to the distant overview; from experience through to analysis.

Part V spends much of its time with Jeannine and with Jeannine and Janet, and contains a number of the performative sections discussed earlier, but 5/XI-XVI are back to Whileway and the observational mode.

Joanna joins Janet on Whileaway in 5/XI (although it is hinted in 5/VI and confirmed in 5/XVII that this is a dream). She sits around the camp-fire, sleeps in the Belin's common room and listens to a story told by a small girl (and translated by Vittoria) about a girl raised by bears. When Joanna realises the story has no end she looks for meaning, only for the child to respond "I tell things… the way they happen". The story is full of exactly the cultural markers that anthropologists look for, that indicate Whileawayans' relationship with nature and with each other: it is both transparent on the surface and opaque to the listener who lacks the cultural references not only for content but for structure. 5/ XII is a beautiful description of the houses and habitations of Whileway, from houses extruded by foam, undersea rookeries and rafts that float in a volcano. Whileaway is a land in which people travel, 'My home is in my shoes' contrasts with *wherever I lay my hat*. This is a nomadic society. Description of homes is followed by illustrative anecdote, gambling with an old woman, seeing a very old statue of an actual man, which has been incorporated into folklore, and this scene (very Jewish), 'If you are so foolhardy as to ask a Whileawayan child to "be a good girl" and do something for you' you will be met with a barrage of questions. There is no unthinking obedience (even the three-quarters-dignity obey only with resentment).

We learn how Whileawayans celebrate, in three sections. In 5/VIII one woman smokes, another reads, another plays notes that transform into music that fill the air and 'By dawn we'll know a little something about the major triad. We'll have celebrated something.' A quiet celebration, a communing. In 5/XIV we see Dorothy Chiliason dancing in a forest glade on her own. Celebration on Whileaway can be solitary, the dances exploratory, 'if a ballet says I Wish… It says I Guess.' It reveals the casualness of the relationship between Whileawayan and intellect. And in 5/XV we have a litany of the things Whileawayans celebrate, some familiar, the solstices, but others encapsulating and communicating to the observer that same intense casualness.

> Happy copulation
> Unhappy copulation
> Longing
> Jokes
> …
> Marriages
> Sport
> Divorces
> Anything at all
> Nothing at all
> Great Ideas
> Death.

The observational scenes have no single rhetoric but when they are considered in clusters one can see the regular use of the trajectory from the intimate to the analytical, from experience through example through summation.

Susan Sniader Lanser argued in 2018,

> 'When narrative theorists talk about voice, we are usually concerned with formal structures and not with the causes, ideologies, or social implications of particular narrative practices. With a few exceptions, feminist criticism does not ordinarily consider the technical aspects of narration, and narrative poetics does not ordinarily consider the social properties and political implications of narrative voice'(5).

This chapter presents Russ as a feminist author who attempts to do just that, and this book as an attempt to analyse the praxis that results; to take on Susan Sniader Lanser's challenge to see narrative technique not simply as a product of ideology but as a vehicle of ideology (5).

Chapter Five: Argument

The Female Man is an argumentative text. It's perhaps the one thing that both fans and hostile critics agree on. The text is polysemous, both because of the four/five voices, but also because

> 'Contained within the representations of women's subjectivity in the book are smaller truth-telling arguments on everything from lesbianism to compulsory heterosexuality… to the fact that women *are not* gentle by nature… All of these smaller truths add to together to support one large truth of the book; these subjectivities, for different women, are all real' (Mandelo 29).

I can't cover everything, but in this chapter I want to explore three of the building blocks of Russ's argument: her Jewishness, her anger, and her humour.[1]

A Jewish text, nu?

Although it is common for critics to observe that Joanna was from a Jewish family, few published critics have considered what this has meant for her writing. Nor have many considered what it means for Jewish readers. This is beginning to change. Melanie Fishbane at the University of Western Ontario was the first to break this silence, with her

---

[1]. I am Jewish, and received a Jewish education, but was raised in a secular home.

2022 PhD paper on Jewish textual embodiment in Russ's work. Valerie Frankel notes that it fed into her feminism and sense of marginalisation (2024); Steven Shaviro has considered its implications for reading *The Two of Them* (2025). But Russ's Jewishness operates at a much more fundamental level, in its structure, and in its anger (which I will discuss in the next section) and importantly, in its argument, which Claire R. Satlof identifies in her discussion of Jewish feminist authors.

In her article 'History, Fiction and the Tradition: Creating a Jewish Feminist Poetic', Satlof argues that Jewish feminist writers such as Esther Broner, Joanne Greenberg, and Cynthia Ozick, 'self-consciously attempt to end the division of the [Jewish] world into a male-controlled spiritual realm and an everyday, profane, women's world' (187). In Russ's Whileaway the spiritual and the profane are interlaced. As we saw in chapter 4, the mundanity of the world of work, is interspersed with an image of a person communing with the mountain or choreographing their own ritual dances. Satloff also points to the degree to which Judaism is a religion of the book and the word, and that Jewish feminism has involved 'the wresting of linguistic control from men and a literary revisioning of Jewish reality' (192). Writing is central to the rebellion of Jewish women, because writing is central to Jewish tradition, and manifests in an 'extreme self-consciousness of the literary form, the constant references to language and literature make clear that these authors are offering an alternative to an inadequate reality' (193) and in an insistence on a remaking and reordering of the world. In addition, Satlof argues that while the work of Jewish American men has been largely realistic, that of Jewish women has partaken of the fantastic. Joanna Russ, not mentioned by Satloff, fits comfortably in this summation.

I am not clear on whether Russ received any Jewish education—that she knew many Jewish men suggests that she was at least brought up in the community—or was active in a Women's Liberation Group; the limited biographical information she appears to have released is unenlightening, although we do know (as discussed in chapter 1) that she was strongly associated with the Jewish-Marxist trade union movement, and in the dedication to Susan Koppelman in *What Are We Fighting For?* (1983), she makes a point of acknowledging Koppelman as a 'fellow Ashkenazy' (an ethnic identity within the world Jewish community).

There is not a great deal obviously Jewish about *The Female Man*. That Joanna's speech patterns are that of a New York Jew may or may or may not create a feeling of familiarity; Joanna's ambitions are those of the Jewish woman wanting what the Jewish man is entitled to: education, and intellectual engagement. But there is the throwaway from Part 1/II...

> Jeannine Dadier (DADE-yer) worked as a librarian in New York City three days a week for the W.P.A. She worked at the Tompkins Square Branch in the Young Adult sections. She wondered sometimes if it was so lucky that Herr Shicklegruber had died in 1936 (the library had books about this). (P1/II)

Which serves as a reminder, if nothing else does, that the Jewish reader has a very different relationship to alternative-war texts than does her gentile colleague. And then there is the opening (or the title) of Book 9

This is the Book of Joanna (9/1)

That bald statement locates the book as one of the Megillot of Jewish tradition (The Song of Songs, Ruth, Lamentations, Ecclesiastes, and Esther), one of the books read on certain festive occasions, two of which front and centre women and the female experience in the male world. Ruth risk everything for her mother-in-law (many feminist writers have seen something empowering in this text); Esther risks everything for her people. The Megillot, though cherished, are also sidelined: they are not allowed to be central to the history of humanity as understood by Jews. In this *The Female Man* is a parallel text, front and centre in its experimentalism which should—but does not—place it among New Wave Texts, and marginalised within the history of science fiction.

We can absolve the gentile-ity of her critics, because Russ herself played down her Jewishness. Russ was far from unique in this. In her 2018 book, *Jewish Radical Feminism*, Joyce Antler, while noting the astonishing proportion of Jewish women in the Women's Liberation movement (the radical wing of the equal rights movement), as many as 40% in the Chicago and New York groups, noted also that these women (Shulamith Firestone, Heather Booth, Amy Kesselman, Vivian Rothstein, Naomi Weisstein and many others) never mentioned their Judaism or associated it with their radicalism. Many of them had grown up in radical left, socialist and secularist Jewish families, but when they joined the New Left, the emphasis on universalism and internationalism (in contrast to modern identity politics) rendered their Judaism irrelevant and, some of them felt, faintly embarrassing. Naomi Weisstein (whose childhood and teens seem to have been relatively similar to those of Russ) felt that there was a whiff of internalised antisemitism in which the pressure to assimilate meant that it was embarrassing to have too many Jews around, or the presence of too many Jews might trigger antisemitism, and the conservatism of many synagogues meant that merging one's activism with one's religion was unlikely (and was to be the project of a later generation, interviewed in the second half of Antler's book).

Several of these radical Jewish women did report experiencing racialised anti-semitism from white men in the New Left. Whatever the cause, according to Antler the result was that Booth, Kesselman, Rothstein and Weisstein, though friends for many years, *never* discussed their Judaism or their identity as Jewish women with each other. In Antler's interviews with these women, however, each retrospectively identified their Judaism as one of the propellants into radical politics: *tikkun olam*, the injunction to repair the world, was a powerful concept for many Jewish radicals of the period.

In entering the secular world, many of these Jewish women found a conflict arising between a Jewish culture that was at once patriarchal yet encouraged women to work, to speak up and to be active and the secular world that was locked into the patriarch 'golden age' of 1950s domestic mythology. Two years younger than Russ, Naomi Weisstein transferred into the Bronx High School of Science to which Russ had been admitted, but not gone due to an unexplained family decision. In her interview with Antler, Weisstein wrote that she hated the place: girls were dismissed, their creativity and intellect and ignored. 'I can still feel my resentment, rage, and despondency at this state of affairs, especially because it seemed as if my future were closing down on me' (39). When Weisstein and her friends entered the New Left movement they experienced the same things: on several occasions when they tried to speak they were told to shut up; some found that they were becoming unable to speak in public. At a major New Left conference Chicago, the National Conference for New Politics, an attempt to put women's liberation issues (abortion, divorce, property rights) on the agenda was rejected by the chair on the grounds that there was already one motion from a women's group (the Women's Strike for Peace). The West Side Women's Liberation Group came directly out of this experience.

Antler asked her subjects about their experience as Jewish women with Jewish men and each identified the same issue: all of them had seen women in their communities as active radicals and active economically, but Jewish men assumed a position of political and intellectual superiority. These women then experienced it again in the New Left. All of them ended up angry, in a culture that validates women's anger rather more than the Christian-secular culture did.

Jewish communities validated intellectual and political aspiration *because* these were the definitions of manly behaviour, as Russ noted in her response to an article in *Lesbian Ethics* (by Julia Penelope, 1986),

> 'No man fixed cars or was athletic in my neighbourhood; no man I knew ever fought physically with another. To the first- and second- generation *shtettle* descendants

around me, what was reserved to men, and what made them superior to women, was not the qualities Julia lists but intellectuality, scholarship and religion... The third-generation Jewish boys I knew at college were quite viciously sexist, but it would never have occurred to them to claim a monopoly on cars or athletics; what they claimed for their own was poetry, philosophy, science and fiction...' (in Russ, 2007, 284).

Paula Hyman concurs:

'Ashkenazi women in Central and Eastern Europe... were traditionally responsible for much of what we would now describe as masculine roles. It was not uncommon, for example, for the Jewish wife to be the primary breadwinner of the family, particularly if her husband was talented enough to devote himself to study' (23).

In Russ's archives there are tantalising hints of Jewishness and what my research assistants, Professors Mary Wood and Karen McPherson note, are references to othering of various groups, in which Jews are loudly NOT mentioned.[2] Other Jewish correspondents, such as Janet Bellweather (Coll. 262, B1, F9), assume Joanna will recognise Yiddish words and phrases; Esther Broner tells a narrative joke about an actor who poses as an astronomer, which is quintessentially Ashkenazi in its poetic and dramatic structure, (Punchline; 'They forgot one thing... that I'm an actor!', 23 June, no year

---

2. My inability to travel to the archives in the summer of 2025 was deeply frustrating, and I am very grateful for Karen and Mary's willingness undertake this task. The notes they sent me, with only the most nebulous of guidance, are the tantalising basis for this paragraph.

but likely 1986, Coll. 262, B1, F9). When Russ is planning to leave Seattle with (presumably) her partner Tracey, she notes that Seattle is very WASP (letter to Michelle Barale, 13 May 1986. Coll. 261, Box 1, F18). Themes of disguise and passing, referenced in a letter to Tiptree, 9 November 1973 (Coll.455/B74/3) crop up regularly in Russ's work, and while often linked to sexuality, also speak to the experience of the secularised Jew, for whom passing through secularised dress and manner can induce guilt, and wariness as it can never be total.[3] One of the most interesting demonstrations of a Jewish sensibility is in Russ's estimation of Le Guin's work which she explored in two letters to Tiptree Jr., 20th August and 14th October, 1976 (Coll. 455. B74, F9).

> 'How can anyone write about anything except life? There isn't anything else. Abstractions grow out of the concretes, and death and life and good and evil are observations made about concrete specifics…Ursula seems to believe (or rather, to feel) that the value and beauty of specifics: characters, places, things, come from their participation in the great abstracts.'

Russ did not enjoy Le Guin's work in part because she felt it was too spiritual. Russ's materialism reflects a religion that, while it has its spiritual aspects, has no heaven or perfection to aim for. It shows up in the work of many Jewish writers where even angels and demons are very earthy (see for example, the work of Isaac Bashevis Singer).

---

3. To the degree Eastern European /Ashkenazi Jews are considered white in post-Holocaust cultures, it often feels conditional, and potential temporary. Liberals may claim they don't see ethnicity (and 'white' Jews have a range of ethnicities) but racists have no such difficulty.

This raises the question, are the J's Jewish? It is noticeable the degree to which each character (as we saw in chapter 3, "Character") is embodied: while the characters are the same genotype, they have been acted upon by their environments and personalities. They move and move through the world differently; they are neither angels, nor (and not even Jael) demons.

Yet the answer is also a clear 'no': Janet cannot be because she lives in a world without reference to Earth religio-cultural systems. We can presume that Jeannine is not because her reference to Herr Shicklgruber (Hitler, who dies in 1936 in this world) is disinterested. Jael *is* a relic of an earth that may be our future, and she is named after the Israelite heroine who killed Sisera, the commander of the Canaanite army. But if Jael is Jewish she is Jewish like Joanna, secularised. Jael meets the author Russ in one way, in Jael's lecture in 9/IX, she explains that in childhood Jael had looked down on 'those girls who were only brought up to be women-women'. Jael and Russ want to be the Jewish man/butch, fighting their battles with intellect and wit. Jael is a fantasy of what it might be like to fight one's battles with violence at a time—after the holocaust—when this was a new thing for Jews (discussed by holocaust survivor Chaim Potok in his novel, *The Chosen*, 1967), to *cut off* argument when it becomes pointless, in chapter 8, by killing the annoying mansplainer. In this, Russ positions herself as very much a part of Jewish radical liberation feminism and we can see this later in this chapter where I have discussed the narratology of anger.

What is also clear to me, and to Melanie J. Fishbane, whose **as yet** unpublished essay I am drawing on here, is that there is also something recognisably Jewish in the structure of Russ's work and particularly in *The Female Man*. Fishbane argues that Russ's experience of a parallel Jewish female culture (the sacred Jewish feminine), and her sense of its underground nature is taken into *The Female Man*. It is not a coincidence that this book is an both an argument and uses argument as its key rhetorical strategy. In 2006 Brian Richardson wrote:

> 'A number of recent works of fiction employ an unidentified, unmarked narrative voice that asks questions that the narrative proper then responds to; for much or all of the text it is not clear what the status of these voices are; whether they emanate from a single source or whether they are irreducibly dual' (Richardson, 2006, 80).

The Female Man asks questions that the narrative proper does not answer, and the status of the voices is fully material and those voices both irreducibly quintupled and reduced to a complex dual voice at the end.

The Female Man is not catechistic, there are no form responses. *The Female Man* is told in four voices and none of them, even the weak voice of Jeannine, is erased. *The Female Man* is very much *pilpul*, that process of argument trained into Jewish men, and which can sound angry to unfamiliar ears because it involves intense textual engagement: 'What [Jewish] men claimed for their own… was poetry, philosophy, science and fiction, all the things I loved the most.' (Russ, *Country you Have Never Seen*, 284). This powers *The Two of Them* and several of the short stories. But her angry narratives are not narratives of silence but of speech. Russ is *not* a woman 'silenced by a masculinist culture' (Romagnolo, 2015, xvii).

There weren't very many ensemble novels around in science fiction in the 1970s: as a genre it was and remains wedded to the individual hero(ine) so the construction of the ensemble is worth considering in Jewish terms. Judaism is a collectivist religion. Although one can say prayers as an individual, much of Judaism revolves around communal engagement, and much of Jewish study is intended to be conducted within the collective space of a yeshiva, often seen as a seminary, but closer to the Buddhist experience of time in a temple in that for many it is a rite of education rather than a route to rabbinical status. The use of four characters in 'discussion' as a mode of story-telling is not dissimilar to that of the rabbis and philosophers of Judaism, but also, given Russ's secular identity, it may map to one of the elements of Judaism that has stayed strongest even among the most secularised of Jews, Passover. In the Passover service, four questions are asked by four fictional sons (this section of the Haggadah is recited by the youngest present): the wise, the wicked, the simple, and the one who is too young/does not know how to ask.[4] This is referenced in 8/VII when Jael takes them 'topside in the branch elevator" The Young One, The Weak One, The Strong One.' (Jeannine, Joanna, Janet?) This maps rather well to the four Js. The four questions of the Pesach service are as follows:

1. **The wise** child asks details about the specific meaning of the laws of Passover observance: 'What are the testimonies, the statutes, and laws which *Adonai* our God has commanded you?' to which

---

4. Taken from ReformJudaism.org: https://tinyurl.com/5n6ft8p3.

we respond with one of the very specific laws of the Passover seder.

2. **The wicked** child asks, 'Whatever does this mean to you?' The authors admonish this child as one who is not concerned about the laws personally, but only for others. This exchange reminds us of the importance of not separating ourselves from our community or from traditions that might seem uncomfortable or foreign to us, but rather to engage with them in ways that enable us to connect with our community.

3. **The simple** child asks, 'What does this mean?' to which a straightforward summary of the story is given, directly from the Torah: 'It was with a mighty hand that God brought us out from Egypt, the house of bondage' (Exodus 13:14).

4. In response to **the child who does not know how to ask**, we are instructed to 'open it up' and explain, 'It is because of what God did for me when I went free from Egypt' (Exodus 13:8).

Janet is the wise child, asking 'what is this?'; Jael, the wicked child, who questions why we are even bothering to ask, but is reminded that she, too, is part of the community of women; Jeannine the simple child, who dreams but still wants to know, which leaves Joanna as the child who does not know how to ask, and in her silence and in her rage she invites us to explain *why*.

Russ's characters struggle to be heard, but none of them has any problem speaking. Janet and Jeannine are both considered in their world rather peaceful and acquiescent characters. Neither ever demonstrate anger but Janet's peacefulness is harnessed to law-keeping whereas Jeannine turns inward; Jeannine's repression of her own anger is destroying her. Jael and Joanna share anger: Jael's anger is harnessed by her society, whereas Joanna has turned it against herself and is within the book, beginning to explore the terror of allowing it to break free

All voices are valid, all voices have something to contribute to the conversation. Fishbane notes that this structure is used in a number of Jewish feminist publications in the 1970s, in *The Women's Haggadah* (1976) and in *Five Books of Miriam: A Woman's Commentary on the Torah* (1997). It also explains why Joanna (the character) is figured not as having a revelation (as a Christian contextualised writer might) but as having an argument with herself and -selves using the intellectual arguments of Joanna and Janet, and the emotions and feelings of Joanna, Jeannine and Jael. One element of the argument of *The Female Man* is that both the lauding of intellectual, 'dispassionate' argument and the dismissal of the power of emotion constructs the world through lies. The extremes of this are both Jeannine and Jael, both of whom are fantasists, but it is Janet who sits in the factually constructed centre, not Joanna who—like Jeannine—careens emotionally between fantasies of liberation and entrapment.

Russ offers *The Female Man* as a challenge to male sf writers in much the same way that the *Feminist Haggadah*, published in 1976, a year after *The Female Man* was a challenge and an intervention. *Tikkun olam*—the injunction to repair the world—is crucial to the structure and argument of *The Female Man*: Janet's is the world already fixed, the other three each broken in their own way; Jeannine still thinking her frustration, her sense of a world already closed off, is her own fault; Laura just beginning to realise that it isn't; and Alice Jael, who wants to destroy her world in order to repair it, while Joanna has not really made up her mind yet but is ready to begin smashing in order to repair.

Pilpul, a method of studying Torah, also shows up here, in the intense study of different engagements between men and women—the creation of performative texts—and the attempt to reconcile (or shatter) the purported links that tie them into a way of being in the world that Russ (and Joanna) reject. Fishbane points to the practice of the study of Midrash, or commentary, which fill in gaps in the principal narrative. The 'shattered' narrative structure of *The Female Man* becomes not a shattering but a construction—a main tale with commentaries around it—if understood in this way, it reverses the figure and ground of the puzzle. Fishbane notes that Midrash readings are communal, not solitary and we can see this too in the construction of *The Female Man*: the four Js are a Midrash group, each analysing the 'text' of the others' worlds, each seeing how their own world is perceived, finding out the rules of the world they inhabit (Russ, 'What can a Heroine Do?', 92).

Finally, the structure of the *humour* is Jewish. The character's tirades are very often self-mocking monologues that ask the author to laugh along with the character, at the character, and at the character's self-mockery. The style is recognisably the Jewish humour of the Borscht Belt, of such comedians as Estelle Getty, Lenny Bruce, Danny Kaye, Jack Benny, Joan Rivers, and more recently, Ruby Wax. The narratives of striving to fit in are familiar to anyone growing up in a fiercely assimilative culture where not to assimilate is to risk death (there are overlaps here with the queer humour of the 1970s).

Rage and Anger

In my introduction to *On Joanna Russ* I argued that there was a joy-in-anger that distinguished Russ's work, and particularly *The Female Man*: I described Russ as a writer who writes with and in anger, whose 'angry creativity burns through the complacent veldt of narrative' (vii). Natalie Haynes has written, 'There are people who dislike thinkers like Beauvoir, because she was angry. Anger, you probably know, is not considered a virtue, and nor is it ladylike' (*Extract from…*, 2015, xiii), a comment which Joanna the ghost might have made. This is probably what is at the bottom of many readers' discomfort with *The Female Man* even where it is a book they admire: anger is frightening, righteous anger even more so. As discussed in chapter 2, anger alienated many male critics. Brian Clark argues (of other Russ books) that Russ is engaged in a 'narrative topology of resistance' (Clark, 25). Its performative structures are precisely an attempt to turn anger from fuel, into a sharpened and well-directed weapon. In the Khatru Symposium in 1975, in the section 'Commentary: Any Freedom That is Granted Can Be Rescinded'[5], Russ argued that women were and are denied anger, not just by men but other women (Le Guin's argument that men and

---

5. This article contains some very strong markers of Second Wave *liberal* feminism that I don't have space to explore but wish to note: first that she argues there is a need for the creation of a female middle class, which she sees as part of the class struggle, a theory I cannot comprehend, and second, under-estimating the retaliation against women; 'The worst thing that might happen… is that feminists… will be harassed, fired from their jobs, punished in various ways, and possibly "lynched" in one way or another' (101). Charnas on p. 94 recognises that this is problematic.

women's anger were equivalent enraged her: 102); 'to think that one can somehow detour around the rage or swallow it or deny it is to cripple oneself. Being treated like Tiny Tim all one's life does indeed induce the most remarkable fury' (Commentary,102). Russ's mission is precisely *not* to convert men, but to whip up women's frustration[6], and to *make it visible*. 'very few men have ever seen a woman really angry. Tears, yes: upset, yes… But rage, rarely, and anger, almost never.' (Commentary, 104) The frustration Russ describes is performed for us by Joanna in many of the early scenes later, as she sees how both Janet and Jael are able to express different kinds of anger, to be transmuted into something golden and glowing.

Although the book begins pleasantly enough with two rather contemplative chapters, Part 3 is an exercise in anger born in frustration. Joanna, the ghost, considers a past in which she would:

dress for the Man
smile for the Man
talk wittily to the Man
sympathize with the Man

In this morass of resentment, Joanna calls up Janet (or does not, depending on whether we accept Janet's story that she is a despatched dimensional traveller). Janet can do things Joanna can't, and for much of the novel Joanna the ghost seeks to restrain (often invisibly) Janet, who is mostly

---

[6]. This probably takes less than Russ assumes. Sarah Gristwood, in *Secret Voices: A Year of Women's Diaries* (2024) found frustration to be the dominant emotion in all women's diaries between 1599 and 2015, so better perhaps to say that Russ sought to turn that frustration into anger.

puzzled by the restraint, rather than angry. For Janet anger is a healthy emotion: she does not understand an anger restrained by fear, nor that one can be anger and not choose or be able to fix the situation that has generated it.

In section 3/II Janet becomes Joanna's alter ego: Joanna dresses resentfully in the restrictive female fashions of the day for a party; Janet strips off the discomfort; Joanna relates a round of 'Ain't It Awful' from the Chorus; Janet wonders at the sense of repetition; Janet refuses to flirt (does not understand that she is being flirted with, or the rules of the game) and when Ginger Moustache begins mansplaining, Janet pushes right back, with knowledge, competence and her own context. When Ewing explains patronisingly that 'most women are liberated right now', that 'You can't challenge men in their own fields', and tries to physically prevent her from leaving, Janet pushes right back, intellectually and physically, despite a background Joanna whispering to her to give way. Where Joanna (in the background) enjoins Janet to back off, Janet pushes back in. One eats their anger, the other will feed it to their opponent to undermine them.

The scene moves from realism to the fabula and back. As it gets more heated it gets more fantastical. The man from Leeds begins to flip through his 'blue book' to find a way to put Janet in her place, 'He said she had acted like a virgin.' Janet, who does not own the pink book, slaps him, not to hurt but as a challenge, and Ewing mutates from new-liberal-faux-feminist into screaming hostility. Janet flattens him. Unfettered by expectation, Janet can express the anger that Joanna (and other women) cannot. Janet can break the scripts in the blue and pink books.

Janet retaliates to known anger-making behaviour the way that Joanna wants to retaliate. Janet retaliates to things that Jeannine knows she hates, but not why, in the way that Jeaninne has never contemplated. In 6/III Jeannine goes to visit her mother and her brother (and his family) in two cottages by a lake. Throughout this section Jeannine is in search of the meaning of happiness. Mrs Dadier (her mother) finds it in doing things, having a 'nice day', a play and a block dance, meeting young people (6/III). Eileen Dadier (6/III) finds it in her conventional marriage and children.

None of Jeannine's family are particularly desirous that she be happy, just that she follows the script. Jeannine is greeted immediately with their demands that she conforms. As she arrives her brother demands, 'When are you going to get married?' (6/III). The ghost watches, and in (6/IV) joins in the exhortation, '"Marry someone who can take care of you", I went on, for her own good. "It's all right to do that; you're a girl…"' Jeannine seethes in misery; she cannot let the misery mutate into anger. Jeannine sits on the porch and as Bud takes her by the arm to introduce her to someone (anyone), Janet emerges into her place. It is Janet that Bud takes by the arm, and Janet who pushes right back. In that second Janet is Jeannine's Id, the Jeannine that Jeannine wants to be, expressing what Jeannine wants to express. But Janet disappears and Jeannine is forced from her reverie of having *choices* at least between men, to her brother's crude and blunt response to who she should marry with 'Anybody' (6/IV). Jeannine swallows her anger once more.

But not all anger is healthy. If Russ asks Jeannine to release her anger, she also asks the reader to consider if women's anger is being directed correctly at men, rather than deflected on to one's fellow woman. The imposition of domestic 'Happiness is brought to its apogee in the Great Happiness Contest' (V) which, it is noted, 'happens a lot'. In this, women compete to swallow their anger while resenting other women who are doing the same. The pattern of the piece is of escalation and then a puncture which breaks the rules of the game, challenging both the dissembling of anger eating, and the misdirection of resentment.

> **FIRST WOMAN**: I'm perfectly happy. I love my husband and we have two darling children. I certainly don't need any change in *my* lot.
> **SECOND WOMAN**: I'm even happier than you are. My husband does the dishes every Wednesday and we have three darling children, each tier than the last. I'm tremendously happy.
> **THIRD WOMAN**: Neither of you is as happy as I am. I'm fantastically happy. My husband hasn't looked at another woman in the fifteen years we've been married, he helps around the house whenever I ask it, and he wouldn't mind in the least if I were to go out and get a job. But I'm happiest in fulfilling my responsibilities to him and the children. We have four children.
> **FOURTH WOMAN**: We have *six* children (This is too many. A long silence.) I have a part-time job as a clerk in Bloomingdale's to pay for the children's skiing lessons, but I really feel I'm expressing myself best when I make a custard or a meringue or decorate the basement.
> **ME**: You miserable nits, I have a Nobel Peace Prize, fourteen published novels, six lovers, a town house, a box at the Metropolitan Opera…
> **All the women: Kill, kill, kill, kill, kill, kill.**

This is anger directed inwards, at that nagging and millennia-long frustration; the anger turned by women at other women, a result of frustration and resentment, is played out again in 6/VI when Jeannine 'is going to put on her Mommy's shoes' and in 6/IX when Jeannine is spending time with her mother, a woman who has drowned her frustrations and anger, and made herself tiny with self-deprecation.

The Great Happiness Contest is followed immediately by a display of anger (and hatred) from a different direction, the anger of the nice liberal man who wants to be seen as an ally and becomes angry with any woman who challenges his veneer.

> He: Why do you think those awful, stupid, vulgar, commonplace women get so awful?
> Me: Well, probably, not wishing to give any offence and after considered judgement and all that, and very tentatively with the hope that you won't jump on — I think it's at least partly your fault.
>
> (Long silence)
>
> He: You know, on second thought, I think bitchy, castrating, unattractive, neurotic women are even worse. Besides, you're showing your age. And your figure's going' (6/V).

These scenes represent the anger that women move through every day.

The anger turned by men on women when women step out of line (in all the many ways that can mean), and that what this means is that there is no way for women to conform or exist in the world as expectation demands, that can possibly be successful or safe, is, of course, the wider topic of the book or, as Russ puts it in one of the funniest, Joan Rivers-style unravelling monologues in the book, the kind that leads Marge Piercy to state of Russ's work: 'Things move along, sometimes with a sense of giddy speed' (viii).

> I know that somewhere, just to give me the lie, lives a beautiful (got to be beautiful), intellectual, gracious, cultivated, charming woman who has eight children, bakes her own bread, cakes and pies, takes care of her own house ...[and etc] holds down a demanding nine-to-five job at the top decision making level in a man's field, and is adored by her equally successful husband because although a hard-driving, aggressive business executive, with eye of eagle, heart of lion, tongue of adder, and muscles of gorilla (she looks just like Kirk Doug-las), she comes home at night, slips into a filmy negligee and a wig, and turns instanter into a *Playboy* dimwit, thus laughingly dispelling the canard that you cannot be eight people simultaneously with two different sets of values. *She has not lost her femininity*. And I'm Marie of Rumania.[7]

This run on section, what Marge Piercy identifies as her jazz improvisatory style (xxi), runs from absurdity to anger, is very funny, and very reminiscent, as I have noted, of the contemporary comedian Joan Rivers, but it remains the anger of frustration, the anger with no clear direction.

---

7. 'Oh, life is a glorious cycle of song,/a medley of extemporanea,/ And love is a thing that can never go wrong,/And I am Marie of Roumania.' Dorothy Parker's father was Jewish and as noted in the text, this humour which flips the trajectory is very Jewish.

Mandelo takes this anger and considers its purpose, and argues convincingly that Russ is engaged in an exercise in *radical truth telling* and that this requires the use of direct address that characterises *The Female Man*. He also argues that the epigraph of 'When it Changed' is the call to arms for *The Female Man*: 'We would have gladly listened to her (they said) *if only she had spoken like a lady*. But they are liars and the truth is not in them.'

That sentence, Mandelo argues,

> 'contains a motivational truth for the stylistic change from subtle and gentle feminism to aggressive, narrative shattering dialectics of radical feminist analysis… to have the truths destroy prior destructive myths, is to be aggressive, to slam doors on their fingers, to punch noses… It is a justification for a novel that, structurally and thematically, is an attack on patriarchy in all its forms' (Mandelo 26).

The Female Man is a Funny Book: Discuss

In *On Joanna Russ* (2009) I discussed Russ's work as burning with anger, and this is true, but it is also witty and often laugh-aloud funny. Russ uses humour to poke fun at the patriarchy, but also (see her essay collection, *Magic Mommas, Trembling Sisters*) at feminism, at feminists, and at herself. Andrew Butler wrote, 'Laughter has largely been located in three overlapping areas: a reaction to incongruity, relief from pent up emotion, and the assertion of superiority' (2009, 151). Butler omits the laughter of fear, and of deflection of danger, although it might be included in relief. This is a humour developed through a need for self-protection, survival and resistance. This section considers three presentations of humour that encourage the reader to laugh, or to recognise a discomfort in laugher: *incongruity*, *appeasement* and *resistance*. Three techniques dominate Russ's demonstrations: bathos (an effect of anticlimax created by an unintentional lapse in mood from the sublime to the ordinary, or the ridiculous), performance, and the monologue and they map quite well on to the three categories.

Incongruity

In part Three of *The Female Man*, we see Joanna use Janet as a critical tool to examine the nature of the interactions she experiences as a woman. The humour is very much at the expense of Joanna who may dislike the routines and compromises she engages with, but is not yet ready for them to be laughed at, for *her* to be laughed at, as if she were a child (or a woman), but it is also at the expense of the reader who brings certain expectation to first-contact novels.

1/IV: The first man to set foot on Whileaway appeared in a field of turnips on North Continent.

1/VII: She said, 'If you expect me to observe your taboos, I think you will have to be more precise as to exactly what they are.' In Jeannine Dadier's world, she was (would be) asked by a lady commentator: How do the women of Whileaway do their hair? JE: They hack it off with clam shells.

There are a number of moments like this which I have pointed out through the text, where a scene is built by Joanna, only to be punctured by Janet with a moment of bathos. Janet is funny and facilitates humour not because we laugh at her, but because Janet refuses to play.

As she prepares Janet for the party, and spins a romantic dream, her thoughts are punctuated with Janet's comment, 'you must remember that to me they are a particularly foreign species; you can make love to a dog, yes? But not with something so unfortunately close to oneself' (3/I).

The other issue for Janet however is that her sense of humour is fundamentally different to that of the other Js. Janet does not laugh at the pain of others, and does not laugh through fear. Her laughter is linked to the absurd: the absurdity of youth and first love; the words of the materialist philosopher Dunyasha Bernadettson; the absurdities of the women who use their five years maternity leave to engage in intense creativity and social engagement; and the absurdities of the old women who work remotely and chatter down the lines at the ills of the younger generation. These things are funny because they are joyous, and we are unused to the laughter of women's joy. Women's laughter is too often self-deprecating: only in recent years (with the rise of comediennes such as Ruby Wax, Jenny Éclair and Jo Brand) have we seen women belly-laugh with pleasure at women's activities. Janet's humour is good-natured and because we are told these things are funny we laugh along with her, with none of the resentment embedded in the other witticisms of the text, nor the assumption that laughter has be to be wielded as a social skill. Which takes us to the laughter of appeasement.

Appeasement

One of the best depictions of the laughter of appeasement in popular culture is the dinner-table scene in *The Death of*

Stalin (Iannucci, 2017): it may be the only media occasion that I've seen where men laugh in fear. For women, laughing to deflect male hostility is common learned behaviour. In *The Female Man* no main character laughs in this way. Jael ignores the jokes of the Man, when they visit Mainland. Jeannine turns away from them, finding them distasteful. Janet is mostly just baffled.

The humour of fear is not the same as 'laughing in the face of danger' which implies a recklessness. The humour of fear is a defence mechanism. *The Death of Stalin* plays on a now common meme: 'Men worry women will laugh at them; women worry that if they don't laugh men will kill them.' Joanna learns this lesson early:

> ... my girl friend's brother indicated the camp counselors' cottages. 'Do you know what those are? "Menopause Alley!" We all laughed. I didn't like it, but not because it was in bad taste. As you have probably concluded by this point (correctly) I don't have any taste; that is, I don't know what bad and good taste are. I laughed because I knew I would have an awful fight on my hands if I didn't. If you don't like things like that, you're a prude ... (6/IV).

The humour of fear is itself funny and we watch the primate seek to appease the dominant [male]. Russ can see that men laugh at women not because they are funny, but to deflect serious commentary: she isn't serious, she's just making a joke, because if it is not a joke the patriarchy crashes and burns. One way to understand *The Female Man* is as an exploration of what humour might look like in a non-patriarchal world where women are free to laugh *because it is funny* and not because they are afraid. So the trajectory of the humour in the novel begins with laughter at men through fear; moves through laughter at the degrees to which women pander to men; Jael *amusing herself* by making a man the joke, and explores through Janet first the humour of incongruity when one of the participants refuses to play, and then what humour without fear might look like.

Joanna fears she herself is ridiculous. In the scenes in which the Greek chorus of Women, pander to the egos of men, she doubles down and in one of the most famous scenes in the book, in 3/II, already quoted here, the women perform exaggerated versions of the ridiculous games that men and women play. The women become figures of fun who charm the manufacture of cars from Leeds (a place that despite his interjection, genteelly, is not genteel), and conspire with him to ridicule feminism.

Andrew M. Butler notes that Janet laughs apologetically when she first meets a man (in 'When It Changed') because she thinks the ritual of shaking hands is so odd (Butler, 2009, 153). But generally, when Janet encounters male arrogance, she does not laugh, because she is not primed to offer the laughter of appeasement. Thus when Ginger Moustache tries to use humour to intimidate and coerce (his charm switching off the second he realises that Janet is not collaborating), he moves quickly into threat.

Joanna intervenes regularly with humour to prevent Janet offending and thus triggering male violence. Janet uses it to humiliate (and provoke?). Jael amuses herself by making a man the joke; in her interaction with the contact in Manland, Jake takes pleasure from feeding the Man the lines he wants, and when he walks into the rhetorical and dialectic trap, kills him, *as a joke*. The others do not laugh,

Jeannine because she is scared, Joanna perhaps because this is something she would really have liked to do, Janet because a messy kill isn't funny. A killer herself, killing is not something to laugh about.

Janet is safe, Janet is strong, Janet is unfearing. But other women are not. In part three Joanna explores what it means to 'dress for The Man/smile for The Man/talk wittily to The Man.../defer to The Man/entertain The Man' etc (3/1). The first three are not separate from the latter. All of this is an act of deference, which actively requires women to look and act in ways which are ridiculous/invite ridicule. Janet punctures this when she uses her lipstick to draw on the walls (as a child might do, unaware of her need to look beautiful but enjoying her own creativity). Joanna acknowledges this when she writes of her physical discomfort in the clothes ordained for the cocktail party: 'My hair feels as if it's falling down, my makeup's too heavy, everything's out of place from the crotch of the panty-hose to the ridden-up bra to the ring whose stone drags it around under my knuckle' (3/II). Everything about the clothing she is wearing seems to ridicule her; it emphasises that this is a role with set lines. She is aware that Janet is on the verge of laughter throughout.

Resistance

Humour though is a powerful tool of resistance; it can be used to deflect threat, and while this is not unique to Jewish Diaspora humour, it is one of the markers of that tradition. Jewish humour has emerged from cultures of fear, in which safety is only ever safety *in this time*. It has emerged from a culture of self-referentiality in which as a group (varied in many ways) we look at ourselves and laugh at the ways in which we seek to accommodate the wider world. While Russ (as I have discussed) was not a religious Jew, she came out of the Marxist Jewish culture of early and mid-twentieth century culture, which we can see expressed in America's early- and mid-century comedians and comediennes.

One scene stands out in this book as part of the humour of resistance, and it is an odd one. In 5/X Russ offers us a parable.

> This book is written in blood…
> Is it written entirely in blood?
> No, some of it is written in tears.
> Are the blood and tears all mine?

Yes, they have been in the past. But the future is a different matter. As the bear swore in *Pogo*[8] after having endured a pot shoved on her head, being turned upside down while still in the pot, a discussion about her edibility, the lawnmowering of her behind, and a fistful of ground pepper in the snoot, she then swore a mighty oath on the ashes of her mothers (i.e. her forebears) grimly but quietly while the apples from the shaken apple tree above her dropped bang thud on her head:

OH, SOMEBODY ASIDES ME IS GONNA RUE THIS HERE PARTICULAR DAY' (5/X).

Walt Kelly, the creator of the *Pogo* comic strip, used animals because he thought they 'hurt less' and it was funnier to hurt them. The same is frequently all too true in

---
8. A comic strip by Walt Kelly which ran from 1948 to 1973.

comedy written by men about women, the assumption is that women hurt less/they're hurt is not real and it's funnier to hurt them.

In *The Female Man*'s Greek chorus scenes, when women enact the scripts men write for them, men both approve and laugh to reward. When women resist these scripts, men disapprove, and laugh to demean. When women fight back, they end up dead. *The Female Man* envisages two alternates: when women laugh, men mock, and women kill them (Jael) and a world in which women laugh *for* women (Whileaway).

But there is another mode of humour in *The Female Man*, and it is the absurdist monologue. In the writing out of behavioural scripts, Russ's anger combines with humour.

> Now in the opera scenario that governs our lives, Janet would have gone to a party and at that party she would have met a man and there would have been something about that man; he would not have seemed to her like any other man she had ever met. Later he would have complimented her on her eyes and she would have blushed with pleasure; she would have felt that compliment was somehow unlike any other compliment she had ever received because it had come from that man; she would have wanted to please that man, and at the same time she would have felt the compliment enter the marrow of her bones; she would have gone out and bought mascara for the eyes that had been complimented by that man...She would have said: I Am In Love With That Man. That Is The Meaning Of My Life. And then, of course, you know what would have happened (3/1).

Or the scene at the party in which Janet is accosted, and quite literally flips the script.

> I want to give you the feeling of the scene. If you scream, people say you're melodramatic; if you submit, you're masochistic; if you call names, you're a bitch. Hit him and he'll kill you. The best thing is to suffer mutely and yearn for a rescuer, but suppose the rescuer doesn't come? 'Let go,——— — —,' said Janet (some Russian word I didn't catch).
> 'Ha ha, make me,' said the host, squeezing her wrist and puckering up his lips; 'Make me, make me,' and he swung his hips from side to side suggestively.
> *No, no, keep on being ladylike!* 'Is this human courting?' shouted Janet. 'Is this friendship? Is this politeness?' …
> '*Savages!*' she shouted. …
> He looked up 'savage' only to find it marked with an affirmative: 'Masculine, brute, virile, powerful, good.' So he smiled broadly. He put the book away.
> 'Right on, sister,' he said.
> So she dumped him. It happened in a blur of speed and there he was on the carpet (3/II).

The fictional Joanna picks up the blue book as he drops it, and compares it to her own, pink one. It instructs the user that, on being denigrated, the woman will promptly break down and acquiesce, accepting it's all her own fault. 'They do fit together so well, you know. I said to Janet: "I don't think you're going to be happy here' (2/II). As the novel proceeds and the voice of Joanna gets stronger, more monologues appear: Laura's on penis envy, about being fobbed off with the proposal that she marry a successful man rather than make the effort to be successful, that she can care for the man, please the man, and generally live for the man (4/XI): in each, the resentment builds to explosion point. There is a monologue of this type in every part after Part 4 and every one of them is funny because it is a monologue that pushes back when women are not expected to push back, that challenges givens.

> Then there is the joviality, the self-consequence, the forced heartiness, the benevolent teasing, the insistent demands for flattery and reassurance. This is what ethologists call dominance behaviour.
> EIGHTEEN-YEAR-OLD MALE COLLEGE FRESHMAN (laying down the law at a party): If Marlowe had lived, he would have written very much better plays than Shakespeare's.
> ME, A THIRTY-FIVE-YEAR-OLD PROFESSOR OF ENGLISH (dazed with boredom): Gee, how clever you are to know about things that never happened.
> THE FRESHMAN (bewildered): Huh? (5/IX).

One of my favourites, that challenges what used to be an absolute given in classrooms, is to the concept of Man. It is the rant we have all women have wanted to give at some point in our educations.

> Years ago we were all cave Men. Then there is Java Man and the future of Man and the values of Western Man and existential Man and economic Man and Freudian Man and the Man in the moon and modern Man and eighteenth-century Man and too many Mans to count or look at or believe. ...If we are all Mankind, it follows to my interested and righteous and right now very bright and beady little eyes, that I too am a Man and not at all a

> Woman, for honestly now, whoever heard of Java Woman and existential Woman and the values of Western Woman and scientific Woman and alienated nineteenth-century Woman and all the rest of that dingy and antiquated ragbag? All the rags in it are White, anyway. I think I am a Man; I think you had better call me a Man ... you will think of me as a Man and treat me as a Man until it enters your muddled, terrified, preposterous, nine-tenths-fake, loveless, papier-mâché-bull-moose head that I am a man (7/VIII).

Writing of *Thelma and Louise*, Kathryn Rowe argues, 'Because women lack acceptable aesthetic or social structures through which to express or even "think" anger, it rarely erupts into the violence or transgressive laughter of *A Question of Silence or Thelma and Louise*.' (1995: Introduction, loc 192/744). Russ is that rarity. The secret of resistance, Russ seems to be saying, is to twist their logic until it weeps. The conceit of the book is to challenge in fiction something Russ posits in *How to Suppress Women's Writing* (1985): 'In a nominally egalitarian society the ideal situation ... is one in which the members of the "wrong" groups have the freedom to engage in literature... and yet do not do so, thus proving that they can't' (4). But Russ goes further, because in *The Female Man*, and in much of her other work (*The Two of Them, We Who Are About to Die*, in particular), she demands that the wrong groups engage not with submission, and acceptance of themselves as marginalised readers and participants, but with anger. Of one critic she noted to a friend, 'I ache for her—because she's young but *where is her anger?*' (Russ, Letter to Susan Koppelman 175). *The Female Man* is intended to stoke anger, but it is also intended to shake apathy (represented by Joanna) and construct hope (represented by both Jael and Janet).

Chapter Six: Epilogue

A coda concludes a story, an epilogue comments or reflects back on it. In his article, 'All is Well: The Epilogue in Children's Fantasy', Mike Madden argues that

> 'The epilogue is not a peritextual feature such as the afterword and the notes, but it is post-narrative despite being narrative. The epilogue is always after but never really outside…the epilogue provides emotional satisfaction. For this emotional clarity and structural removal, it has the feel of a fable's moral' (Cadden, 345).

Cadden argues that the epilogue reassures, but that it is a risky strategy, a breaking of the closure and the immersion in the tale (345). *The Female Man* has already broken the fourth (and several other) walls by Part 9, but here, it does something different, in that, until section VII, it may, by offering analysis, even go in closer to the narrative.

This is an epilogue about the epilogue, an afterword about the afterword. Part 9 is presented both as story, and external to the story. It brings together the story and creates a point of poise from which new directions are thrown (John Clute's 'slingshot ending' characteristic to science fiction, see the Science Fiction Encyclopaedia online) and as Pat Rogers (1992) has suggested of epilogues, they loosen the *temporal screw* allowing the characters to jump forward in time in a novel that has been loose in both place and time, but surprisingly well bound in terms of connection. Joanna-the-narrator who has previously mostly lurked in the background, comes front and centre.

The structure of the epilogue seems almost random (as does, at times, the novel as a whole), but while this does not work literally, there is a degree to which it can be seen as a Markov chain, in which each event depends only on the event just prior to it: first the identity *as the Book of Joanna*, moving into the scene of the boy and his father performing patriarchal aggression (II), the exploration of the compass of knowledge and what women know (III); the revolutionary act of shutting a door on a man's thumb (V); learning to despise oneself (V); the revolutionary act of making love to a woman (VI); to the last section (VII).

The epilogue spins out like the Fibonacci spiral and in doing so the style of delivery changes. In the introduction I noted that *The Female Man* is almost entirely paratactic in its syntax. Only in the conclusion to the book does this change in a frenzy of hypertaxis that generates a sense of 'emotional clarity and structural removal' (Cadden 345).

This is the book of Joanna (9/I).

With this statement, and as Melanie Fishbane posited, Russ positions her epilogue as a Megillot, a biblical aside to the narrative of the people of Israel, or in this case, just the people. Where the Book of Ruth informs the story of King David and the Israelites, *The Female Man* talks to the narrative of egalitarian America and to the 'meritocratic' world of science fiction, and the ameliorative world of Second-Wave Feminism. The Book of Joanna is a story that tells us about ourselves. Joanna the character begins to merge with Joanna the author, over a period of seven 'parts', in what Felicity Nussbaum called the double consciousness, that has lurked in this book; Joanna is the traditional female epilogist who challenges the integrity of the narrative. 9/II Joanna drives on a four-lane highway, admiring buttercups. The boy child in the car sees it as a race, 'Beat 'im!' He cries, objecting when Joanna falls back behind a car instead of passing. It's a child's game, however aggressive, but the father frames it as a gender war: 'Joanna drives like a lady.' The boy, in training, learns that his excitement and aggression are manly.

Joanna reflects on the gender divide and the way that men construct a faux compassion in which their interests and passions are beyond you, because women don't care about such things, or if they do, they aren't proper women, and the way that politics is a game in which women's lack of interest is seen as natural, a reflection of female incapacity and not as a product of its lack of relevance. 'No squabble between the Republican League and the Democrat League will ever change your life. Concealing your anxiety over the phone when He calls; that's your politics' (9/III).

9/IV begins with the first revolutionary act, the deliberate shutting of a door on a man's thumb: this is the scene that most upsets male reviewers because, unlike Jael killing the boss, it's real, it makes you wince. The act of deliberately hurting, of not being kind, is the most radical act in the book, and it flags the key radical position; she is not petty, she is uncaring. Women are not supposed to be uncaring. From there the section segues into the litany of observation; women make up just one-tenth of the [visible] world, the default of any role is to male. Women can be mothers, waitresses, teachers, secretaries and nuns, but most of those evaporate on marriage (it's 1969, not 1975 when the book was published). So if women don't exist, then they are just making a fuss for nothing. Women live circular lives, from girl to mother, from sacrificed for, to sacrifice 'you begin to wonder if the whole thing isn't a plot to make the world safe for (male) children. There is no space for women...' There is no space in which to be female; one must continually be selfless. The sequence proceeds through point and counterpoint but concludes with the young Joanna, unselfconsciously engaging in experiment, thinking very well of herself as an exception and yet...

9/VI begins with a fairy tale, in which Brunhild hangs her husband on a nail but is disempowered by sex. It moves to the child Joanna, empowered by unselfconsciousness and misprision of the world around her. Child-Joanna-World is Barbie-world, in which her mother is President, women rule the world and men serve them. It is an ironisation of the narrative sold to little girls. But Laura Rose is younger, she stands outside this. She has already discovered that there is both a get-out clause and a curse in the adjudication that she is different. She attracts Joanna and we see Joanna as both material and ghost, hovering, fantasising, trying to negotiate those fantasies, wanting, fearing, and finally kissing. Both of them hot and awkward, and Joanna resenting that now she will be told that her resentment and rage is because she is a Lesbian. And counterpoint that she cannot call herself a lesbian because she likes sex with men, because her partner is a friend, all the reasons which lead lesbian identity and activity to be discounted.

The very final section(9/VII) begins with a last look at Jeannine, who has much of Joanna, yet is not. Jeannine is saying 'goodbye to all that', a phrase taken from the title of Robert Graves' 1929 autobiographical account of the First World War: both salutation and memorial. She says goodbye to material objects that tell her how to be, to ideologies that still try to trap her, or engagements with capital letters that tell her how to live or how not to live, and says hello to politics with a small p that are relevant to her life, and to a focus on women, and the (to both Jeannine and Joanna) new reliance on women's friendship for validation.

The women meet at Schrafft's, a well known New York eatery which specialised in feeding working women and shopping women the kind of light food that contemporary men were taught to sneer at. Jael negotiates for a base for Womanland and is accepted by Jeannine and rejected by Janet, their alternate perspectives foil(ed) by Janet's dislike of the food, Jael's pleasure in it.

The section segues into a positioning of each of them as everywoman, each are also Joanna. And Janet in weeping for Jael and the ultimate outcome of the gender war, weeps for us.

The women pay the bill and leave, and the book, perhaps the only real narrator, says goodbye in a stream of thesis and antithesis:

It begins, 'Goodbye, goodbye, goodbye' and is followed by two clearly differentiated paragraphs. In the first, each of the three Js is summed up: Alice Reasoner, who says 'die if you must but loop your own intestines around the neck of your strangling enemy' (9/VII); Janet 'who we don't believe in and whom we deride... Radiant as the day, the Might-be of our dreams, living as she does in a blessedness none of us will ever know..', and Jeannine, 'poor-once-as-I-was'. Russ has created a trinity of Femaleness to replace Maiden, Mother and Crone.

> Goodbye to Alice Reasoner [Jael],
> who says tragedy makes her sick, who
> says never give in but always go down
> Fighting [...]
> Goodbye to Janet, whom we don't
> believe in and whom we deride but
> who is in secret our savior [...]
> Goodbye, Jeannine, goodbye, poor soul,
> poor girl, poor as-I-once-was.

The epilogue draws to a close, 'I'm God's typewriter and the ribbon is typed out.'

The narrative plot of *The Female Man* is not 'self-regulated', the structure does not 'maintain' or 'close itself' (Chatman, 21). There is a closure of a kind: Alice Jael Reasoner makes a deal with Jeannine that her world can be a refuelling base for Jael's world (but as we promptly leave that narrative space there is no *consequence* depicted, Mendlesohn, 2009) but the narrative does not close with story closure, instead it *transforms* into a flash forwards or sideways that breaks the wall or proscenium arch of the story. An exercise in Utopia as praxis (Moylan, 82) the epilogue forces us to identify with and acknowledge our place as audience, and the story as narrated; to acknowledge what Chatman argues is 'narrative as a communication' (28) with a sender and a receiver.

But Cadden also argues, 'It may be true that a sense of completion is *more* important than narrative closure"

(346) which Russ demonstrates in 9/VII. The women go to Schrafft's. They go to a women-only place, sit down in a women-only space, talk about controlling the world, they make agreements, they pay the bill, they go. Ordinary yet—because it involves only women and all have agency—is revolutionary, a small whiff of Whileaway.

Shlomith Rimmon-Kenan argues that in the present day 'suggestiveness and indeterminancy are preferred to closure and definitiveness' (61); we can see this in the epilogue of *The Female Man*. The structure of the epilogue is also very Jewish, there is no heavenly goal, no eschatological transformation, no sense of healing at the end. Instead, this novel of argument ends in disagreement: Jael is in search of a base, but only two of the others accept. Janet also refuses Jael's explanation of Whileaway.

The lessons Jael brings, Joanna has already learned; the world Janet tells of is both unreachable and yet it can be reached. If Cadden is correct that, 'The distance between beginning and end is measured by a sense of cause and effect' (Cadden, 355) then for a slim book, the distance between beginning and end is huge. The book is a stone thrown into a still pool to create a ripple that will upend the world.

The book concludes with its final, triumphal despatch, directed not at the reader, but at the book itself, "Go, little book....!" A phrase that originated in Ovid, came to English via Chaucer and was used by Spenser and Milton. Joanna Russ, a Professor of English Literature, is actively positioning the text in the tradition of English Literature.

Go little book... to trot through the states, to curtsey at the shrines of foremothers, to be polite, to be humble and unassuming, 'Not to scream when you are ignored, for that will alarm people...' to be ladylike as the book itself is not, to *stay hopeful* which it is. Not to worry if it becomes 'quaint and old fashioned'.

And thus, it is with mixed feelings that I note that the final words of the epilogue remain as appropriate as ever.

Do not get glum when you are no longer understood, little book. Do not curse your fate. Do not reach up from readers' laps and punch the readers' noses.
Rejoice, little book! For on that day, we will be free.

Acknowledgments

Thank you to members of the British Science Fiction Association who nominated a talk for a non-fiction award despite its roughness and gave me encouragement when I really needed it; and to my employers, the Association of Charity Independent Examiners, who were incredibly kind in 2020, and who have been unfailingly supportive, if a bit baffled. Thank you also to the NHS: readers don't need details, but the staff of the NHS saved my life three times in 2020. Without them, you would not be reading this book.

All of my work has built on the work of others: so grateful thanks to Jed Hartman and Nichole Rudick who shared their research in the Joanna Russ papers, in Eugene, Oregon; Melanie Fishbane, and Steven Shaviro for insightful work on Joanna Russ and Judaism; Robin Anne Reid, for very helpful pointers and her extensive knowledge of feminist sf criticism; Ken MacLeod for identifying US Marxists for me. The vagaries of MLA are such that one does not list everything one has read, so if you expect to see your work referenced in the bibliography and it's not, please be assured I did read and appreciate it.

My beta readers and invaluable critics of this manuscript were: Melanie Fishbane, Christopher Owen, Joy Sanchez-Taylor, Audrey Taylor, and Paul Weimer. Mary Wood and Karen McPherson acted as researchers in the University of Oregon archives for me when a trip to the United States became inadvisable. Edward James proof-read and indexed the book.

The cover of this book is the artwork Judith Clute created for the Women's Press Book Club edition of *The Female Man*. Judith and I have been friends for several decades now (my, time flies) and I am so delighted to be able to have my favourite cover of my favourite science fiction novel, created by one of my closest friends, on the cover of this critique.

Thank you also to Francesca T. Barbini, editor-owner of Luna Press Publishing for taking this book so that it can retail at an affordable price.

And then there is Edward James, as always, for believing in my work, and for looking after me during perhaps the worst eighteen months of my life.

Index

Again, Dangerous Visions (ed. Ellison) 10, 39
Alice Jael Reasoner: see Jael
And Chaos Died... 4-5, 17, 38
anger 141-148
Antler, Joyce 130
appeasement , humour of 150-153
Aristotle 7, 18, 47, 54
Attebery, Brian 91
Bakhtin, Mikhail 91
Bammer, Angelika 30-31, 34, 53
Banker, Amelia 35
Bannon, Anne 83
Barbour, Douglas 47
Bart, Pauline 17
bear, the 108, 154
Beauvoir, Simone de 141
Bernard, Jessie 36, 37
biological essentialism 26-27, 32, 43-43
Booth, Wayne C. 59, 90, 91
Booth, Heather 130
Boulter, Amanda 27
Bradley, Marion Zimmer 32
Brecht, Bertolt 15, 54,59,73,87,108
Broner, Esther 128, 133
Bronte sisters 44-45
Bujold, Lois McMaster 116
Butler, Andrew M. 148, 152
Butler, Judith 115
Butler, Octavia 32
Cadden, Michael 165, 166
Calvin, Ritch 48
Carter, Angela 25
Chatman, Seymour 98, 165
Chaucer, Geoffrey 166
Chernin, Kim 17
Clark, Brian 141
Clute, John 54, 160
Clute, Judith 49, 50

Cohn, Dorrit 59, 76, 105
Coney, Michael G. 30, 42
Conklin, Groff 14
Cortiel, Jean 3, 43, 51, 52, 57, 58, 86
Csicsery-Ronay Jr, Istvan 12-13
Dadier, Mrs 72, 73, 111, 114, 144
Dalloway, Mrs (see also Woolf) 9, 66
Daly, Mary 36, 37
Death of Stalin, The 150-151
Del Rey, Lester 46
Delany, Samuel R.4-5, 13, 17, 32, 43
   Trouble on Triton 5
Delorey, Denise 9, 72
Depression, The 2, 91
Di Filippo, Paul 58
Duchamp, L. Timmel 24
Dunyasha Bernadetteson 119, 150
Dwivedi, Divya 56
ectoplasmadiegetic 58, 65
Edwards, Malcolm 48
Elgin, Suzanne Haden 32
Elliott, Beth 31-32
English girls' school stories 42
epilogue 160
Ewing (character) 64, 111, 143
Female Man, The (Russ)
   as Gothic 53
   as utopia 4
   audience for 22
   covers of 49-51
   publication of 38, 43
   quarantined 8
   reactions to 46-49
   transphobia of 25-27
female writers of SF 15
feminism 1, 15, 17, 18, 19, 22-23, 27, 28, 29,31, 35, 36, 52, 64, 69, 111, 128, 135, 141, 148, 152, 161
Feminist Haggadah 139

feminist SF criticism 35-36
Firestone, Shulamith 19-20, 24, 36, 37, 69, 130
Fishbane, Melanie J. 127-128, 135-136, 161
Frankel, Valerie 128
Fraser, Clara 17-18
Friedan, Betty 44
Fry, Stephen 67
Frye, Joanna S. 5, 39-40, 85
Futurians, the 17
Gearhart, Sally M. 4, 25
Geis, Richard E. 30
Genette, Gérard 95
Gernsback, Hugo 16
ghost 3, 65, 72, 74, 76, 87-88, 144
ghost stories 52
ghoul 87, 88, 105
Gilman, Charlotte Perkins 4, 52-53
Ginger Moustache 64, 111, 143, 152
Gollancz 48, 50
Goodwin, Michael 46
Gopal, Priyamvada 6
Graves, Robert 164
Great Happiness Contest 73, 113, 146
Greek Chorus 3, 7, 22, 54, 108, 111, 152, 155
Grendel's mother 116
Grimwood, Jon Courtenay 67
Gristwood, Sarah 14, 142
Hacker, Marilyn 46
Harter, Richard 46
Hartman, Dominic 51
Haynes, Natalie 141
Hicks, Heather J. 33-34
Hitler, Adolf 2, 67, 135
Hogan, Kristen 47
Home Economic 45
Horsely, Lee 24
housewife heroines 24, 30, 35
How to Suppress Women's Writing (Russ) 10, 16, 31,45, 158
humour 7-8, 148-159
incongruity, humour of 149-150
Jael (Alice Jael Reasoner, character) 2-3, 6, 51, 52, 53, 57, 58, 75, 86, 87-91, 97, 102, 106-107, 135, 164
Jahn, Manfred 67-68
James, Edward 1, 16, 46
Janet (Janet Evason, character) 2, 3, 6, 40, 52, 57, 58, 60-66, 77, 78, 79-80, 86, 88, 97, 98, 99, 100, 101, 102, 105, 142-144, 149-150, 153, 164
Jeannine (Jeannine Dadier, character) 2, 3, 6, 24, 52, 57, 58, 61, 66-75, 76, 81-82, 83-84, 86, 88, 89, 97, 98, 99, 100, 103, 104, 135, 144, 149, 165
Jetée, La 101
Jewish culture 127-140
Jewish humour 7-8, 140, 153-154
Joanna (character) 2, 52, 57, 58, 61, 63, 64, 65, 72, 74, 75-87, 89-90, 97, 99, 100, 102, 104, 142-143, 152-153
Jones, Gwyneth 15, 33, 36, 38, 43,46, 52, 106
Judaism 21-22, 85, 128, 131, 137
Juhasz, Suzanne 10
Katz, Stephanie 56, 91, 95
Kelly, Janis 47, 51
Kesselman, Amy 130
Khatru Symposium 6, 14, 45, 141
Koppelman, Susan 36, 129, 158
Kristeva, Julia 93
Lanes, Mary 4
Lanser, Susan Sniader 95, 98, 126
Larbalestier, Justine 29
Le Guin, Ursula K. 30, 36, 39, 43, 134, 141-142
Leeds, Man from 111, 143, 152
LeFanu, Sarah 5, 33, 39, 40, 41, 45, 51
Leinster, Murray 101
Lorde, Audre 7
Lundwall, Sam J. 29
Lynn, Elizabeth 47
Man, the concept of 157-158
Mandala, Susan 6, 11
Mandelo, Brit 28, 51-52, 127, 148
Manland 3, 26, 38, 89, 90, 152
mansplaining 110, 143
March-Russell, Paul 94

Marcus, Laura 47-48
Marie of Rumania 147
Marxism 4, 6, 17, 18, 22, 23, 28, 43, 129, 154, 168
Matson, Patricia 11-12
McClenahan, Catherine 48, 54
McIntyre, Vonda N. 33
McPherson, Karen 133
Megillot 85, 130, 161
Mendlesohn, Farah 1, 10, 14, 28, 32
Merrick 8, 42
Merril, Judith 29, 36
metaphor 5, 7, 9-11, 52, 53, 64, 66
Metaphors We Live By (Lakoff and Johnson) 10-11
Mezei, Kathy 9, 12, 76, 85-87
Mill, John Stuart 115
mise-en-scène 96-97, 118-121
modernism 9
Moles, David 27
monologues 34, 75, 97, 109,114-115, 121, 140, 147, 156
Morgan, Robin 31-32
Moylan, Tom 3, 4, 34, 43, 48, 94, 165
Nussbaum, Felicity 162
observational 96, 121-126
Ovid 166
Panshin, Cory and Alexei 46
paratactic language 7, 9, 11, 161
Parker, Dorothy 147
Passover 137-138
Penelope, Julia 132
performance 96, 108-118
Peyton, Rog 46
Picnic on Paradise (Russ) 16, 37-38
Piercy, Marge 8, 33, 147
pilpul 136, 140
Pogo 108, 154
Pollak, Alec 8, 13, 27
postmodernism 34-35, 58
Potok, Chaim 135
Purser, Autun 50
Radway, Janice 69
resistance, humour of 153-159
Richardson, Brian 68, 75, 85, 98, 136

Richeson, Clee 51
Rimmon-Kennan, Shlomith 96, 121, 166
Rivers, Joan 140, 147
Rosinsky, Natalie M. 8
Rothstein, Vivian 130
Rowe, Kathryn 158
Rudick, Nichole 29
Russ, Joanna
    and theatre 15-16
    education of 13-15
    Jewishness of 22, 26, 127-140
    political development of 17-19
    transphobia of 25, 31-32
    writing career of 15-17
Sargent, Pamela 33
Satlof, Claire R. 128-129
Schaefer, Kate 13, 18
Schopenhauer, Arthur 105
Schrafft's 92, 107, 165
Second Wave feminism 23, 25, 141
Second World War 2, 15, 69, 70
sex 2, 30, 62, 68, 91, 106, 123, 163
Sex Class dialectic 20
SFWA 15
Shaviro, Steven 128
Singer, Isaac Bashevis 134
Smith, Jeffrey 6
Solnit, Rebecca 110
Spare Rib 1
Stanzel, Franz K. 66
Star Trek 14
Stockwell, Peter 9-10
story 96, 97-107
subaltern criticism 6
theatre 16, 74, 78, 108
Thelma and Louise 158
Tiptree Jr, James (Alice Sheldon) 10, 14, 19, 21, 33, 34, 39, 45, 134
transphobia 25, 27, 32
Tristram Shandy (Sterne) 95
Trump, Donald 115
Tuttle, Lisa 25
Two of Them, The (Russ) 5, 14, 20, 128, 136,158
We Who Are About To… (Russ) 20, 45, 158

Weisstein, Naomi 15, 130, 131-132
What Are We Fighting For? (Russ) 17, 19, 25, 129
'When It Changed' (Russ) 16, 20, 30, 39, 40, 41, 42, 66,148, 152
Whileaway 2, 4, 6, 8, 19, 20, 41,51, 54, 57, 60, 62, 63, 70, 92, 101, 118-120, 124-125
Wilding, Laura Rose 86, 102, 114, 122, 123,156, 163
Wilhelm, Kate 33
Wittig, Monique 4, 30-32, 92
Wolfe, Gary K. 36
Womanland 3, 38, 107, 164
women in police force 40, 41
Women's Press Book Club 1, 47
Wood, Mary 133
Wood, Susan 47
Woolf, Virginia 9, 11, 12, 24, 72, 87
Yaszek, Lisa 4, 14, 29, 30, 35
Zoline, Pamela 30, 71

Russ's Critical Works Cited

Russ, Joanna. '*Amor Vincit Foeminam*: The Battle of the Sexes in Science Fiction.' *To Write Like a Woman*. Bloomington and Indianapolis: Indiana University Press, 1995. 41-60. Print.
—. *The Country You Have Never Seen: Essays and Reviews*. Liverpool: Liverpool University Press, 2007. Print.
—. *How to Suppress Women's Writing*. The Women's Press, 1984. Print.
—. 'Is "Smashing" Erotic?' *To Write Like a Woman: Essays in Feminism and Science Fiction*. Bloomington and Indianapolis: Indiana University Press, 1995. Print.
—. 'Letter to Susan Koppelman.' *To Write Like a Woman: Essays in Feminism and Science Fiction*. (1984) Bloomington and Indianapolis: Indiana University Press, 1995. 171-76. Print.
—, ed. *Magic Mommas, Trembling Sisters, Puritans & Perverts*. Trumansberg, New York: The Crossing Press, 1981. Print.
—. 'Ms Russ and Mr Delany.' *Wiscon*. Ed. Delany, Samuel R. Broad Sheet, 2006. Print.
—. 'On "the Yellow Wallpaper".' *To Write Like a Woman: Essays in Feminism and Science Fiction*. Bloomington and Indianopolis: Indiana University Press, 1995. 159-66. Print.
—. 'Recent Feminist Utopias.' *To Write Like a Woman: Essays in Feminism and Science Fiction*. Bloomington and Indianapolis: Indiana University Press, 1995. 133-48. Print.
—. 'Sf and Technology as Mystification.' *To Write Like a Woman. Essays in Feminism and Science Fiction.* Bloomington and Indianapolis: Indiana University Press, 1995. 26-40. Print.
—. 'Somebody's Trying to Kill Me and I Think It's My Husband: The Modern Gothic.' *To Write Like a Woman: Essays in Feminism and Science Fiction*. Bloomington and Indianapolis: Indiana University Press, 1995. 94-119. Print.
—. 'Speculations: The Subjunctivity of Science Fiction.' (1973). *To Write Like a Woman*. Bloomington and Indianapolis: Indiana University Press, 1995. 15-25. Print.
—. 'This Is Your Life.' *Khatru Symposium: Women in Science Fiction*. Ed. Jeffrey Smith, 1995. 62-66. Print.

—. 'To Write "Like a Woman": Transformations of Identity in the Work of Willa Cather.' *To Write Like a Woman: Essays in Feminism and Science Fiction.* Bloomington and Indianapolis: Indiana University Press, 1995. 149-58. Print.
—. *To Write Like a Woman: Essays in Feminism and Science Fiction.* Bloomington and Indianapolis: Indiana University Press, 1995. Print.
—. 'Towards an Aesthetic of Science Fiction' (1975) *To Write Like a Woman: Essays in Feminism and Science Fiction.* Bloomington and Indianapolis: Indiana University Press, 1995. 3-14. Print.
—. *What Are We Fighting For?: Sex, Race, Class and the Future of Feminism.* New York: St. Martin's Press, 1998. Print.
—. 'What Can a Heroine Do? Or Why Women Can't Write.' *To Write Like a Woman: Essays in Feminism and Science Fiction.* Bloomington and Indianapolis: Indiana University Press, 1995. 79-93. Print.

Works Cited: Secondary Sources

Abate, Michele Ann. *Tomboys: A Literary and Cultural History*. Philadelphia: Temple University Press, 2008. Print.

Abbot, H. Porter. *The Cambridge Introduction to Narrative*. Cambridge: Cambridge University Press, 2008. Print.

Antler, Joyce. *Jewish Radical Feminism: Voices from the Women's Liberation Movement*. New York, NY: New York University Press, 2018. Print.

Attebery, Brian. *Fantasy: How It Works*. Oxford: Oxford University Press, 2022. Print.

Bammer, Angelika. *Partial Visions: Feminism and Utopianism in the 1970s*. New York and London: Routledge, 1991. Print.

Bart, Pauline. *Nice Jewish Girls: A Lesbian Anthology*. Ed. Beck, Evelyn. Torton, Washington, DC: Labrys Books, 2023. Print.

Booth, Wayne C. *The Rhetoric of Fiction*. Chicago: The University of Chicago Press, 1981. Print.

—. *The Company We Keep: An Ethics of Fiction*. Berkeley, Los Angeles: University of California Press. 1988. Print.

—. 'Resurrection of the Implied Author: Why Bother?' *A Companion to Narrative Theory*. Eds. Phelan, James and Peter J. Rabinowitz. Oxford: Blackwell Publishing, 2008. 75-88. Print.

Boulter, Amanda. 'Unnatural Acts: American Feminism and Joanna Russ's *The Female Man*.' *Women: A Cultural Review* 10 (1999): 151-66. Print.

Brody, Miriam. 'Introduction and Notes.' *Mary Wollstonecraft: A Vindication of the Rights of Woman*. Ed. Miriam Brody. Harmondsworth: Penguin Books, 2004. Print.

Broner, E. M., and Naomi Nimrod. *The Women's Haggadah*. San Francisco: Harper, 1986. Print.

Butler, Andrew. 'On Joanna Russ.' *On Joanna Russ*. Ed. Mendlesohn, Farah. Middletown, CT: Wesleyan University Press, 2009. 143-56. Print.

Cadden, Michael. 'All Is Well: The Epilogue in Children's Fantasy Fiction.' *Narrative* 20 (2012): 343-56. Print.

Calvin, Ritch. '"This Shapeless Book": Reception and Joanna Russ's *The Female Man.*' *Femspec* 10.2 (2010): 24-34. Print.

Chatman, Seymour. *Story and Discourse: Narrative Structure in Fiction and Film*. Ithaca and London: Cornell University Press, 1978. Print.

Clark, Brian Charles. 'The Narrative Topology of Resistance in the Fiction of Joanna Russ.' *On Joanna Russ*. Ed. Mendlesohn, Farah. Middletown, CT: Wesleyan University Press, 2009. 225-38. Print.

Clute, John. '*The Two of Them*, by Joanna Russ.' *Foundation: the Review of Science Fiction* 15 (January, 1979): 103-05. Print.

Cohn, Dorrit. *Transparent Minds: Narrative Modes for Presenting Consciousness in Fiction*. Princeton, New Jersey: Princeton University Press, 1978. Print.

Cortiel, Jeanne. *Demand My Writing: Joanna Russ/Feminism/Science Fiction*. Liverpool: Liverpool University Press, 1999. Print.

—. 'Joanna Russ: *The Female Man.*' *A Companion to Science Fiction*. Ed. Pringle, David: Blackwell, 2005. 500-11. Print.

Csicsery-Ronay, Jr., Istvan. *The Seven Beauties of Science Fiction*. Middletown, CT: Wesleyan University Press, 2008. Print.

Currie, Mark. *About Time: Narrative, Fiction and the Philosophy of Time*. Edinburgh: Edinburgh University Press, 2007. Print.

Davin, Eric Leif. *Partners in Wonder: Women and the Birth of Science Fiction 1926-1965*. Lanham MD et al: Lexington Books/Rowman & Littlefield, 2006. Print.

De Beauvoir, Simone. *Extracts from the Second Sex*. Ed. Reid, Martine. London: Vintage Books, 2015. Print.

Del Rey, Lester. 'War of the Sexes.' *Analog: Science Fiction, Science Fact*. 95.6 (1975): 166-70. Web.

Delany, Samuel R. 'Joanna Russ and D. W. Griffith.' *On Joanna Russ*. Ed. Mendlesohn, Farah. Middletown, CT: Wesleyan University Press, 2009. 185-96. Print.

Delany, Samuel R. *Starboard Wine: More Notes on the Language of Science Fiction*. Middletown CT: Wesleyan University Press, 2012 (c. 1994). Print.

Delorey, Denise. 'Parsing the Female Sentence: The Paradox of Containment in Virginia Woolf's Narratives.' *Ambiguous Discourse: Feminist Narratology and British Women Writers*. Ed. Mezei, Kathy. Chapel Hill, NC: University of North Carolina Press, 1996. 93-108. Print.

Dow, Bonnie J. *Watching Women's Liberation, 1970: Feminism's Pivotal Year on the Network News*. Urbana, Chicago and Springfield: University of Illinois Press, 2014. Print.

Duchamp, L. Timmel. 'Old Pictures: The Discursive Instability of Feminist SF." *Extrapolation* 45 (1) (2004). 15-33. Print.

Dwivedi, Divya. 'The Addressee Function, or the Uses of Narratological Laity: Lessons of Khasak.' *Narratology and Ideology: Negotiating Context, Form, and Theory in Postcolonial Narratives*. Ed. Dwivedi, Divya, and Richard Walsh. Columbus, OH: Ohio State University Press, 2018. Print.

Firestone, Shulamith. *The Dialectic of Sex: The Case for Feminist Revolution*. London: The Women's Press, 1979 (c.1970). Print.

Fishbane, Melanie J. 'The Book of Joanna: Jewish Textual Embodiment in Joanna Russ's *The Female Man*.' 2023. Print. Unpublished Thesis. Western University, Canada.

Frankel, Ellen. *Five Books of Miriam: A Woman's Commentary on the Torah*. Harper One, 1997. Print.

Frankel, Valerie Estelle. *The Post-Holocaust Authors, Foreword by Jack Dann*. Lanham, MD: Lexington Books, 2024. Print.

Fraser, Clara. *Revolution, She Wrote*. Seattle: Red Letter Press, 1998.

Frye, Joanne S. *Living Stories, Telling Lives: Women and the Novel in Contemporary Experience*. Ann Arbor: The University of Michigan Press, 1986. Print.

Genette, Gerard. 'Order, Duration and Frequency.' *Narrative Dynamics: Essays on Time, Plot, Closure and Frames*. Ed. Richardson, Brian. Columbus, OH: The Ohio State University, 2002. 25-24. Print.

Goodwin, Michael. 'One Giant Step for Science Fiction.' *Mother Jones*. I.VI (1976): 62-3. Web.

Gopal, Priyamvada. 'Reading Subaltern History.' *The Cambridge Companion to Postcolonial Literary Studies*. Ed. Lazarus, Neil. Cambridge: Cambridge University Press, 2004. 139-61. Print.

Gristwood, Sarah. *Secret Voices: A Year of Women's Diaries*. 2024. Print.

Hacker, Marilyn. 'Science Fiction and Feminism: The Work of Joanna Russ.' *Chrysalis* 4 (1977): 67-69. Print.

Harter, Richard. 'Science Fiction Is Trash.' *Richard Harter's World* (1998). Web.

Hicks, Heather J. 'Automating Feminism: The Case of Joanna Russ's

Female Man.' Post Modern Culture 9 (3) (1999). Print.
Hughes, Kathryne. *The Short Life and Long Times of Mrs. Beeton*. Harper Perennial, 2005. Print.
Hutcheon, Linda. *A Poetics of Postmodernism: History, Theory, Fiction*. London and New York: Routledge, 1988. Print.
—. 'Coda. Incredulity toward Metanarrative: Negotiating Postmodernism and Feminisms.' *Ambiguous Discourse: Feminist Narratology and British Women Writers*. Ed. Mezei, Kathy. Chapel Hill, NC: University of North Carolina Press, 1996. 262-67. Print.
Hyman, Paula. 'The Jewish Family: Looking for a Useable Past.' *On Being a Jewish Feminist: A Reader*. Ed. Heschel, Susanna. New York Schocken Books, 1995. 19-26. Print.
Jahn, Manfred. 'Focalization.' *The Cambridge Companion to Narrative*. Ed. Herman, David. Cambridge: Cambridge University Press, 2007. 94-108. Print.
Katz, Stephanie. *Here We Go Round in Circles: The Definition of Circular Narrative as a New Narrative Typology*. PhD dissertation, University of Birmingham, 2022.
Kristeva, Julia, and Leon S. Roudiez, eds. *Desire in Language; a Semiotic Approach to Literature in Art by Julia Kristeva*. New York: Columbia University Press, 1980. Print.
Lanser, Susan Sniader. *Fictions of Authority: Women Writers and Narrative Voice*. Ithaca and London: Cornell University Press, 1992. Print.
Larbalestier, Justine. *The Battle of the Sexes in Science Fiction*. Middletown, CT: Wesleyan University Press, 2002. Print.
Le Guin, Ursula K., et al. 'SF Is Suited to the Needs of Any Group That Feels Itself Oppressed.' *Khatru Symposium: Women in Science Fiction* (1975). Ed. Smith, Jeffrey 1993. 6-10. Print.
Le Guin, Ursula K., et al. 'That's a Girl?' *Khatru Symposium: Women in Science Fiction* (1975). 1993. 11-17. Print.
Lefanu, Sarah. *In the Chinks of the World Machine*. London: The Women's Press, 1988. Print.
—. 'Introduction.' *To Write Like a Woman: Essays in Feminism and Science Fiction*. Bloomington and Indianapolis: Indiana University Press, 1995. Print.
Mandala, Susan. *Language in Science Fiction and Fantasy: The Question*

of Style. London: Continuum, 2010. Print.

Mandelo, Brit. 'Queering Sff: *The Female Man* by Joanna Russ (+ Bonus Story, 'When It Changed').' *Tor.com* (2011). Web.

—. *On Joanna Russ and Radical Truth Telling*. Conversation Pieces. Seattle, WA: Aqueduct Press, 2012. Print.

March-Russell, Paul. 'Art and Amity: The "Opposed Aesthetic" in Mina Loy and Joanna Russ.' *On Joanna Russ*. Ed. Mendlesohn, Farah. Middletown, CT: Wesleyan University Press, 2009. 168-84. Print.

Marcus, Laura. 'Feminism into Fiction: The Women's Press.' *Times Literary Supplement* 27 September 1985. Print.

Matson, Patricia. 'The Textual Politics of Virginia Woolf's *Mrs. Dalloway*.' *Ambiguous Discourse: Feminist Narratology and British Women Writers*. Ed. Mezei, Kathy. Chapel Hill, NC: University of North Carolina Press, 1996. 162-86. Print.

McClenahan, Catherine. '"Textual Politics": The Uses of the Imagination in Joanna Russ' *The Female Man*.' *Transactions of the Wisconsin Academy of Sciences, Arts and Letters* 70 (1982): 114-25. Print.

Mendlesohn, Farah. 'Introduction.' *On Joanna Russ*. Ed. Mendlesohn, Farah. Middletown, CT: Wesleyan University Press, 2009. vii-xi. Print.

—. *The Inter-Galactic Playground. A Critical Study of Children's and Teens' Science Fiction*. Jefferson NC and London: McFarland, 2009. Print.

—. 'The Unravelling Narratives of James Tiptree Jr.' *ContactZone* 1 (2023): 62-71. Print.

Merrick, Helen. 'The Female "Atlas" of Science Fiction? Russ, Feminism and the Sf Community.' *On Joanna Russ*. Ed. Mendlesohn, Farah. Middletown CT: Wesleyan University Press, 2009. Print.

—. *The Secret Feminist Cabal: A Cultural History of Science Fiction Feminisms*. Seattle: Aqueduct Press, 2009. Print.

Mezei, Kathy. 'Introduction. Contextualizing Feminist Narratology.' *Ambiguous Discourse: Feminist Narratology and British Women Writers*. Ed. Mezei, Kathy. Chapel Hill, NC: University of North Carolina Press, 1996. 1-20. Print.

—. 'Who Is Speaking Here? Free Indirect Discourse, Gender, and Authority in *Emma*, *Howards End*, and *Mrs. Dalloway*.' *Ambiguous Discourse: Feminist Narratology and British Women Writers*. Ed.

Mezei, Kathy. Chapel Hill, NC: University of North Carolina Press, 1996. 66-92. Print.

Moylan, Tom. *Demand the Impossible: Science Fiction and the Utopian Imagination*. New York and London: Methuen, 1986. Print.

Newell, Dianne, and Jenea Tallentire. 'Learning the "Prophet Business".' *On Joanna Russ*. Ed. Mendlesohn, Farah. Middletown, CT: Wesleyan University Press, 2009. Print.

Panshin, Alexei, and Cory Panshin. 'Review of *The Female Man*', *The Magazine of Fantasy and Science Fiction*. August 1975, Volume 42: 46-53. Print.

Penelope, Julia. 'Heteropatriarchal Semantics and Lesbian Identity: The Ways a Lesbian Can Be.' *Lesbian Ethics* 2: 58-80. Print.

Piercy, Marge. 'Foreword.' *The Zanzibar Cat*, by Russ, Joanna: Arkham House Publisher Inc., 1983. vii-xii. Print.

Pollak, Alec. 'Introduction: I'm Not a Girl I'm a Genius.' *On Strike against God*. Ed. Pollak, Alec. New York: The Feminist Press, 2024. Print.

Radway, Janice. *Reading the Romance: Women, Patriarchy, and Popular Literature*. London and New York: Verso, 1984. Print.

Rich, Adrienne. 'Split at the Root.' *Nice Jewish Girls: A Lesbian Anthology*. Ed. Beck, Evelyn Torton. Washington DC: Labrys Publishing, 2023. 73-90. Print.

Richardson, Brian. *Unnatural Voices: Extreme Narration in Modern and Contemporary Fiction*. Columbus, OH: The Ohio State University Press, 2006. Print.

—. 'Beginnings and/as Endings.' *Narrative Beginnings: Theories and Practices*. Ed. Richardson, Brian. Lincoln: University of Nebraska Press, 2008. 91–94. Print.

Rimmon-Kenan, Shimon. *Narrative Fiction*. New Accents. London and New York: Routledge, 2002. Print.

Rogers, Pat. 'The Parthian Dart: Endings and Epilogues in Fiction.' *Essays in Criticism* 42 (2), 1992, 85–106. Print.

Romagnolo, Catherine. *Opening Acts: Narrative Beginnings in Twentieth-Century Feminist Fiction*. Lincoln: University of Nebraska Press, 2015. Print.

Rowe, Kathleen. *The Unruly Woman: Gender and the Genres of Laughter*. Austin: University of Texas Press, 1995. Print.

Rudick, Nicole, ed. *Joanna Russ: Novels and Stories*. Literary Classics of the USA, New York: The Library of America, 2023. Print.

Russ, Joanna, et al. 'Commentary: Any Freedom That Is Granted Can Be Rescinded.' *Khatru Symposium: Women in Science Fiction* (1975). Ed. Smith, Jeffrey1993. 101-11. Print.

Russell, Charles. *Poets, Prophets and Revolutionaries: The Literary Avant-Grade from Rimbaud through Postmodernism*. New York and Oxford: Oxford University Press, 1987. Print.

Said, Edward 1. *Beginnings, Intention and Method*. Baltimore MD: Johns Hopkins University Press, 1975. Print.

Satlof, Claire R. 'History, Fiction, And the Tradition: Creating a Jewish Feminist Poetic.' *On Being a Jewish Feminist*. Ed. Heschel, Susanna. New York: Schocken Books, 1983. 186-207. Print.

Shaviro, Steven. 'On (Not) Saving the World: Joanna Russ's Extra (Ordinary) People.' *Jewish Women Science Fiction Writers Create Future Females*. Ed. Barr, Marleen. Lanham MD: Lexington Books, 2025. 39-63. Print.

Smith, Jeffrey, and Joanna Russ. 'Gimmicks Are Not Enough.' *Khatru Symposium: Women in Science Fiction* (1975). Ed. Smith, Jeffrey1993. 60-61. Print.

Stanzel, Frank. *A Theory of Narrative*. Cambridge: Cambridge University Press, 1986. Print.

Stockwell, Peter. *The Poetics of Science Fiction*. Harlow, Essex: Longman, 2000. Print.

Wolfe, Gary K. 'Alyx among the Genres.' *On Joanna Russ*. Ed. Mendlesohn, Farah. Middletown, CT: Wesleyan University Press, 2009. 3-18. Print.

Woolf, Virginia. 'A Room of One's Own.' *A Room of One's Own and Three Guineas*. Ed. Barrett, Michele. Harmondsworth: Penguin, 1993. 3-103. Print.

Yaszek, Lisa. 'A History of One's Own: Joanna Russ and the Creation of a Feminist SF Tradition.' *On Joanna Russ*. Ed. Mendlesohn, Farah. Middletown, CT: Wesleyan University Press, 2009. 31-47. Print.

www.ingramcontent.com/pod-product-compliance
Lightning Source LLC
LaVergne TN
LVHW011828060526
838200LV00053B/3938